ESSENTIAL MANAGERS

# P[illegible] PERFO[illegible] THROUGH NLP

JOHN SEYMOUR & MARTIN SHERVINGTON

**Senior Editor** Nina Hathaway
**Senior Designer** Jamie Hanson
**DTP Designer** Julian Dams
**Production Controllers** Alistair Rogerson, Michelle Thomas

**Managing Editor** Adèle Hayward
**Senior Managing Editor** Stephanie Jackson
**Senior Managing Art Editor** Nigel Duffield

Produced for Dorling Kindersley by

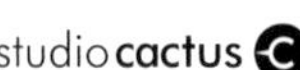

13 SOUTHGATE STREET WINCHESTER HAMPSHIRE SO23 9DZ

**Editor** Kate Hayward
**Designer** Laura Watson

First published in Great Britain in 2001 by
Dorling Kindersley Limited,
9 Henrietta Street,
Covent Garden, London WC2E 8PS

2 4 6 8 10 9 7 5 3 1



A CIP catalogue record for this book is available from the British Library

ISBN 0 7513 1291 6

Reproduced by Colourscan, Singapore
Printed and bound in Hong Kong by Wing King Tong



# CONTENTS

## Helping Others Improve

## Continuing to Improve

# INTRODUCTION

*The ability to develop good relationships with others and to handle situations effectively are vital elements of being a successful manager. Introducing the skills of NLP (Neuro-Linguistic Programming),* Peak Performance Through NLP *helps you to recognize the cues that give you insights into how you and others are feeling, and develop the way you approach situations so that you can achieve the highest standards. By identifying areas of your performance that you need to improve, NLP focuses on changing your thoughts, assumptions, and emotions so that you can dramatically improve the results you get. Practical advice, including 101 concise tips, shows you how to develop NLP skills and put them into practice, and a self-assessment test at the end of the book allows you to evaluate your performance levels.*

# THINKING ABOUT PERFORMANCE

NLP (Neuro-Linguistic Programming) helps managers to work well with others and to develop themselves. Use NLP to recognize the small changes that produce significantly better results.

## KNOWING THE KEY SKILLS

*The critical factor for maximizing professional performance is improving how you manage yourself and your working relationships with others. Recognize that this is something you can learn and that NLP shows you how to develop the necessary skills.*

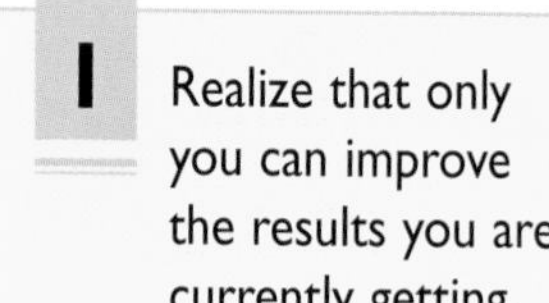

1
Realize that only you can improve the results you are currently getting.


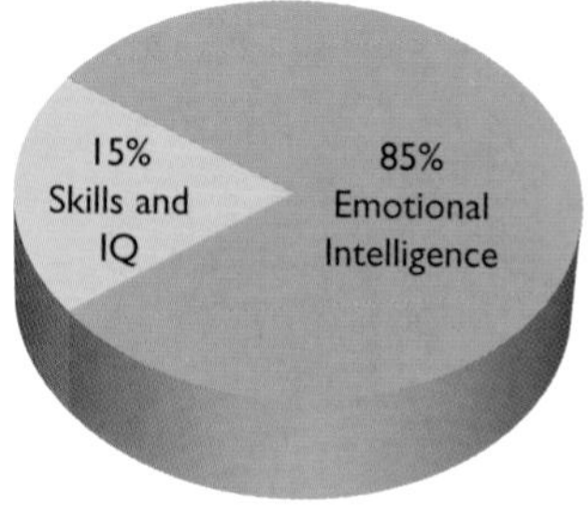


▲ **IDENTIFYING SUCCESS**
*Technical skills and IQ account for about 15 per cent of top-level performance, whereas 85 per cent of professional success is due to emotional intelligence.*

### IMPROVING EFFECTIVENESS

Globalization and improved communication technologies have increased the pressure on all businesses to perform, and this in turn has put pressure on staff performance. Recent research has shown that it is not primarily IQ or technical competence that determine your professional effectiveness. The biggest impact on professional success is how well you manage yourself and your working relationships with others – known as "emotional intelligence". Increase your effectiveness as a manager by identifying and developing the critical emotional intelligence skills you need.

### Points to Remember

- Poor performers will often feel stress and react in a less than optimal way.
- When you have a problem, think about the skills you could learn to increase your competence.
- It is important to be curious about what your emotions are trying to tell you.

## Understanding Emotional Intelligence

There are two aspects of emotional intelligence that determine your performance as a manager. The first is your ability to handle situations in an effective manner. Top performers use their emotions as a guide to improving what they do. The second is your ability to be sensitive to others and knowing how to make a difference to the performance of others.

## What Is NLP?

The field of NLP is a "tool kit" of skills used by managers to develop emotional intelligence skills and improve performance. NLP skills focus on the way you think about what you are doing that already works, what you are doing that does not work, and what you need to do differently. Change what you think, feel, and believe, and you will dramatically alter the results you get. With repeat practice, these skills become automatic and lead to a continuous improvement in performance.

**2** Understand that emotional intelligence can transform your performance and career.

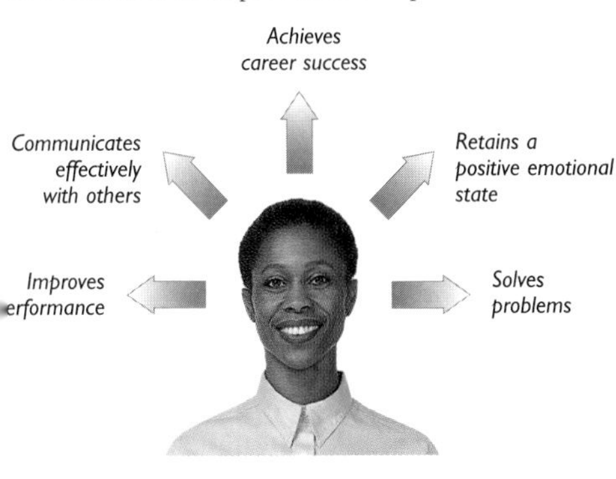


▲ **APPLICATIONS OF NLP**

*By adopting NLP skills, you can quickly increase your effectiveness and significantly improve your performance. This has an impact on the results you and your organization achieve.*

## Using NLP

Many people think that emotional intelligence is a natural skill that you either do or do not have. It is, in fact, a set of skills that you can learn. Use NLP techniques to help you identify and focus on areas of your performance that you need to improve. Then, explore what to do differently, so that you can begin to improve the results you achieve. This is the first step in developing your emotional intelligence.

# APPLYING NLP SKILLS

**M**uch of your performance at work is probably already very effective. However, applying NLP skills will help you improve the small part of your work that limits your overall performance. Many of the skills in NLP will be natural to you already, such as goal-setting or mental rehearsal. Once you are aware of an area where you do not perform well, choose an NLP technique that will make a difference to your performance. If, for instance, you realize that you have difficulty meeting important deadlines, use the NLP skill of setting yourself daily objectives so that you are able to plan your time effectively.

**3** Recognize that NLP focuses on what works.

**4** Look at your work and identify any difficulties.

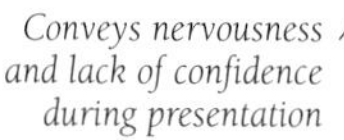

Gives an assured and effective presentation

Conveys nervousness and lack of confidence during presentation

**USING MENTAL REHEARSAL TO IMPROVE YOUR PERFORMANCE ▲**

*This manager recognizes that he is nervous when giving presentations to his colleagues. Through using the NLP skill of mental rehearsal, he could improve his performance considerably.*

### Questions to Ask Yourself

**Q** What areas of my performance am I satisfied with?

**Q** What aspects of my performance do I want to improve?

**Q** Do I know what I need to do to improve my skills?

**Q** What is the first action step I need to take to improve my results?

## Focusing on Process

NLP skills are also used for problem solving. NLP looks at the content of issues or communications, while also looking at their structures or processes. For instance, it is not what someone says, but how they say it that tells you how to respond. The words spoken are the "content" of a conversation, whereas the "process" of communication is far broader. It includes all of the non-verbal messages. For instance, "That's great!" can mean opposite things depending on the context and how it is said. Learn to be flexible in your approach and assumptions.

## Assumptions to Adopt for Peak Performance

| Positive Assumptions | Reasoning |
|---|---|
| If what you are doing is not working, do something different. | If you always do what you have always done, you will always get what you have always got. |
| There is no failure, only feedback. It is what you do with results that matters. | Whatever happens, you can use feedback to make improvements to results. |
| People can access the resources they need to make whatever changes will make a difference. | There is always something that makes a difference, and it is usually inner resources. |
| We each create our own version and view of reality. | We perceive the world through our senses and create different models of reality. |
| It is easier to change yourself than it is to change others. | Changing what you do will change others' responses to you. |
| Using your imagination is the first stage to making real improvements. | Improvements begin as thoughts, are communicated in words, and become actions. |

# BOOSTING CONFIDENCE

*Top-level performance requires high levels of confidence, especially in demanding circumstances. Take responsibility for how you feel and, when you need to boost your morale, use NLP techniques to develop the skill of maintaining confidence.*

**5** Realize that you can easily learn to build your self-confidence.

**6** Avoid blaming yourself for problems, since this lowers your self-confidence.

## SEEING YOUR ACHIEVEMENT

You may imagine the worst scenario in a situation. Thinking about potential problems is only useful if you imagine how best to deal with them. The difference between a confident and a non-confident person is their ability to imagine performing tasks well. The better you are at imagining your own successes, the better your self-image and the higher your level of self-confidence. Keep imagining your own successes until they feel "true".

## AVOIDING BLAME

In any specific task, your abilities are related to your levels of confidence and competence. Your level of competence is often not a problem, but people lose confidence when things go wrong and then competence can fall. Your reaction may be to blame yourself or others. Realize that blaming others lowers their confidence and also damages your relationship with them. Instead, think what you could more usefully say. Then, notice how the confidence level of yourself and others improves.

### DOS AND DON'TS

- ✔ Do believe you are good enough.
- ✔ Do practise talking confidently.
- ✔ Do focus on your successes.
- ✔ Do encourage and praise good work.

- ✘ Don't dwell on problems.
- ✘ Don't stamp out creativity.
- ✘ Don't criticize the performance of others.
- ✘ Don't assume your staff cannot improve.

**7** Practise imagining yourself doing a task well, such as giving effective and constructive feedback.

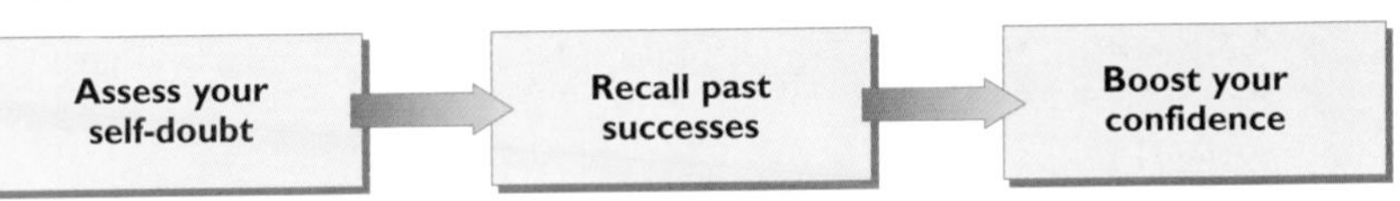
Assess your self-doubt
Recall past successes
Boost your confidence

▲ INCREASING YOUR CONFIDENCE

*Explore any self-doubt and then recall a past experience that contradicts this doubt. Imagine yourself behaving with this past confidence in the future and you will boost your present confidence.*

### QUESTIONS TO ASK YOURSELF

**Q** Are there any occasions in the past when I was a confident decision maker?

**Q** Do I praise my team and pay them compliments for work that has been done well?

**Q** Have I examined the areas where I lack confidence?

## BUILDING CONFIDENCE

Work on building your confidence. Believe in yourself and your abilities, assume you will find solutions, and feel good about outcomes. Any belief to the contrary will reduce your confidence. For example, if you believe you are a poor decision maker you will feel unconfident about decisions. Look for these barely-conscious limiting beliefs and weaken them by finding an exception. Recall a past experience that contradicts this belief and imagine yourself behaving decisively.

**8** Remember your experiences of peak confidence.

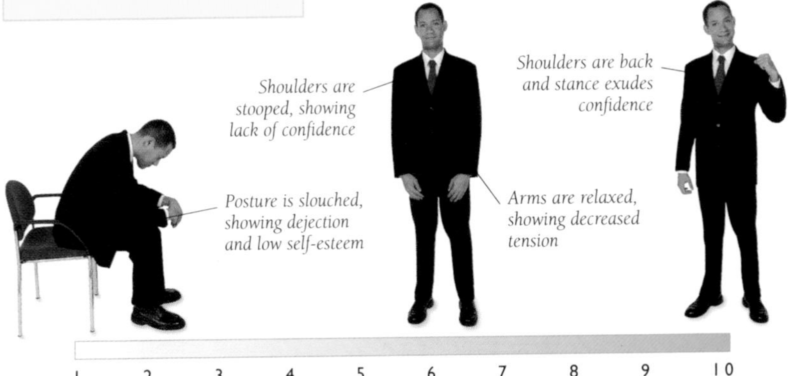
Shoulders are stooped, showing lack of confidence
Posture is slouched, showing dejection and low self-esteem
Shoulders are back and stance exudes confidence
Arms are relaxed, showing decreased tension
1
2
3
4
5
6
7
8
9
10

SCALING CONFIDENCE LEVELS ▲

*Rate your level of confidence on a scale of one to 10. Imagine dropping it by a point, to make yourself feel less confident. Now increase it by two points. Notice the change in your posture and mind. Repeat this exercise to boost your confidence.*

**9** Maintain a positive image of yourself in the future.

# SETTING YOUR OBJECTIVES

*The process of setting objectives helps you to think through complex and changing situations. Avoid reactive "fire fighting" and use goal-setting skills. Realize that, as the skills become natural, you will find managing problems and change easier.*

**10** Set clear goals and outcomes to get the results you want.

## PLANNING OUTCOMES

All successful people are clear about their goals and aims. Even though you may already set yourself goals, make sure that you use this skill regularly so that you can maximize your performance. Set goals many times a day, making sure they are achievable. Every outcome is made up of sub-outcomes, so identify the sub-outcomes as steps to achieving peak performance. For example, people improve their communication skills (sub-outcomes) in order to improve results (outcome).

◀ **SOLVING PROBLEMS**
*All effective people use a version of outcome thinking regularly as a solution-focused technique for planning, and for dealing with problems or crises.*

## KNOWING WHEN TO PLAN

As well as developing the habit of planning your objectives thoroughly, learn to know when to think about them. Firstly, use outcome thinking every time you are planning ahead, whether it is prioritizing with a simple "to-do" list, or in strategic organizational planning. Secondly, use outcome thinking to deal with unexpected problems as they arise. Ask yourself, "Which is the central problem here?" and then run the issue through the outcome POWER model (see opposite) until you are clear about the next action step.

**11** Remember, you can achieve more if you set goals.

**12** Develop the habit of thinking about outcomes.

## USING THE POWER MODEL TO SOLVE PROBLEMS AND PLAN EFFECTIVELY

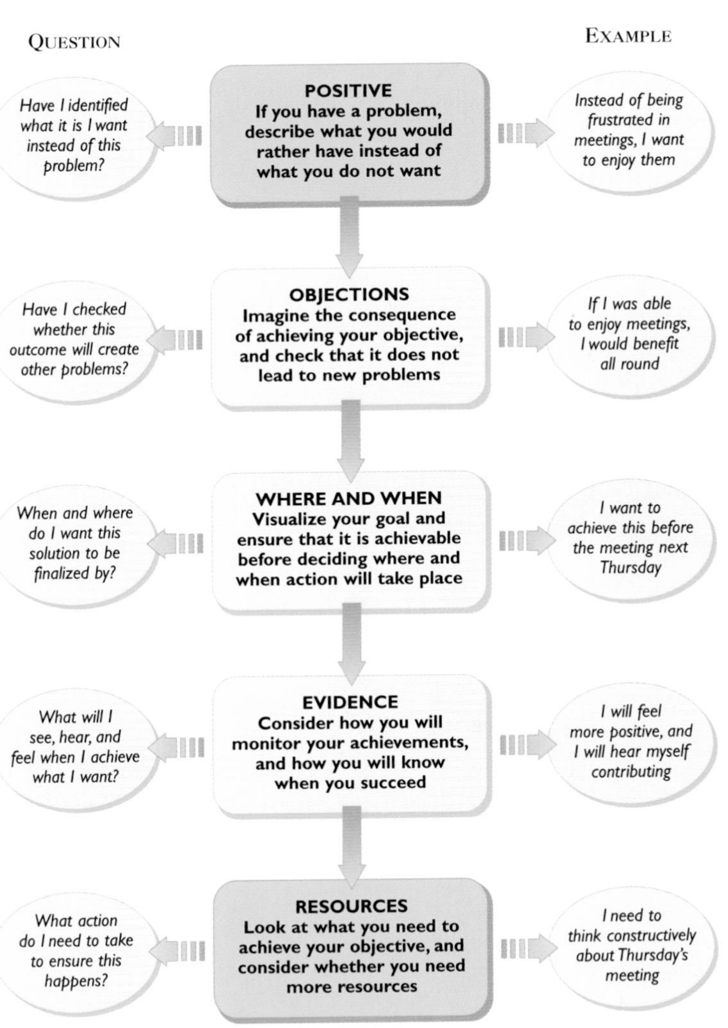

QUESTION
EXAMPLE
Have I identified what it is I want instead of this problem?
POSITIVE
If you have a problem, describe what you would rather have instead of what you do not want
Instead of being frustrated in meetings, I want to enjoy them
Have I checked whether this outcome will create other problems?
OBJECTIONS
Imagine the consequence of achieving your objective, and check that it does not lead to new problems
If I was able to enjoy meetings, I would benefit all round
When and where do I want this solution to be finalized by?
WHERE AND WHEN
Visualize your goal and ensure that it is achievable before deciding where and when action will take place
I want to achieve this before the meeting next Thursday
What will I see, hear, and feel when I achieve what I want?
EVIDENCE
Consider how you will monitor your achievements, and how you will know when you succeed
I will feel more positive, and I will hear myself contributing
What action do I need to take to ensure this happens?
RESOURCES
Look at what you need to achieve your objective, and consider whether you need more resources
I need to think constructively about Thursday's meeting

# MANAGING PERSONAL FLEXIBILITY

*Your results are determined by the way you manage yourself internally. Increase your awareness of the changes you can make in how you approach situations in order to develop the inner flexibility needed for outstanding performance.*

**13** Imagine how someone you respect would view a problem.

**14** Be flexible in your approach to other people.

**15** Adapt your approach to match particular people.

## INCREASING FLEXIBILITY

Top performers choose the right methods to produce outstanding results. Develop the mental flexibility to generate high-quality options so that you can pick the best one. Think through possible approaches until you know which one is likely to work best. If you have difficulties, ask yourself, "What is the best way to view this situation?" For example, instead of viewing a colleague as "difficult", see them as a challenge. Develop your flexibility by thinking of different approaches to situations. Aim to achieve the best from others.

## MAKING CHANGES

Your approach to situations is determined by your internal world – your thinking (T), assumptions (A), and emotional state (E). If you change one of these, you will change how you perceive and deal with a situation. For instance, if you have too much work, you may see only the negative points – you may be frustrated because you assume that it is not negotiable. Instead, decide which aspect of your approach is the easiest to change. You could focus on the positive (T), assume you can renegotiate (A), or feel motivated instead of frustrated (E).

### THINGS TO DO

1. Watch how other people respond to you.
2. Make a note of the interactions that work.
3. Examine your thoughts, moods, and assumptions, and look at what you could change.

# CHANGING YOURSELF

Develop the flexibility to handle situations at work by changing aspects of your feelings, beliefs, and thoughts. First, when you are in a difficult situation, check your emotional state and, if necessary, work on improving it. For example, remember a situation in which you did feel positive and imagine being back in it for a few seconds. Second, check your assumptions. Is what you are assuming true? Third, check your thinking. Is there a way of thinking about the situation that works better than your current approach?

### ▼ MAKING CHANGES

*By changing any aspect of your inner world, you change the results you get. In this example, the way the manager behaves affects his employee's behaviour and directly effects the results he achieves.*

*Manager asks constructive questions*

*Problem is quickly resolved*

*Approaches employee to find out what happened*

*Manager receives a customer complaint*

*Manager is confrontational and employee becomes defensive – issue is not resolved*

**16** Think through possible approaches until you find the best option, and then proceed to take action.

# IMPROVING YOUR PERFORMANCE

As you focus on your performance, you will notice an improvement in your results. Develop your NLP skills so that you can begin to achieve better work relationships.

## LEARNING HOW TO LEARN

*Top business performance comes from having a wide range of competencies. Recognize the key skills you need to focus on, consider how you will develop them, and learn to use the technique of mental rehearsal to consolidate what you learn.*

**17** Be responsible for your performance, so that you can improve it.

**18** Invest in your future success by developing skills.

**19** Understand that management skills can be mastered using NLP skills.

### MANAGING PERFORMANCE

There are three main areas of performance management, which include many different skills. Focus on the area you most need to work on:

- Self-management skills: These include goal setting and managing time. Your management skills will grow out of how you manage yourself.
- Project-management skills: Develop these so that you know what needs to be done and when, so you can keep projects on track.
- People-management skills: Recognize that it is your ability to communicate effectively with people that determines the success of projects.

## KNOWING WHAT TO LEARN

Focus on a problem you have and decide which skill you need to develop in order to overcome the issue. For example, something that upsets you is an indication that you need to develop your emotional self-management skills. Be clear about what you are trying to achieve. If you want to remain calm in this situation, look at how to achieve this. In this case, the skill you need to learn is emotional stability.

**Unconscious incompetence:** You are unaware of a skill

↓

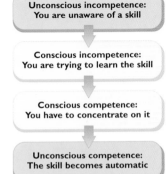

**Conscious incompetence:** You are trying to learn the skill

↓

**Conscious competence:** You have to concentrate on it

↓

**Unconscious competence:** The skill becomes automatic

THE LEARNING MODEL ▶

*This is the process of learning a new skill so that, at each stage, you have a higher level of competence. You move from unconscious incompetence to the mastery of unconscious competence.*

## TAKING ACTION

Improve your performance by focusing on only one key skill at a time. Choose and prioritize the area which has the biggest impact on your performance. Put time in your diary to clarify the specific skill needed, for example, interpersonal skills. Then, use this time to decide the actions you are going to take to develop this skill, for example, arranging a series of coaching sessions.

◀ TAKING THE TIME TO LEARN

*Setting aside time for self-improvement is the only way to improve your performance. Remember that nothing is more important than developing your management skills.*

## REHEARSING SITUATIONS

Use repeated mental rehearsal to build skills quickly. Imagine dealing with situations better. If you find this difficult, think of someone you know who deals with situations well. Notice what they do differently and imagine yourself working in that way. For example, if you are overloaded with work, you will remain overloaded unless you know what to change. Practise thinking how you will react differently the next time someone overloads you.

**20** Practise responses mentally until your new response is word perfect and becomes automatic.

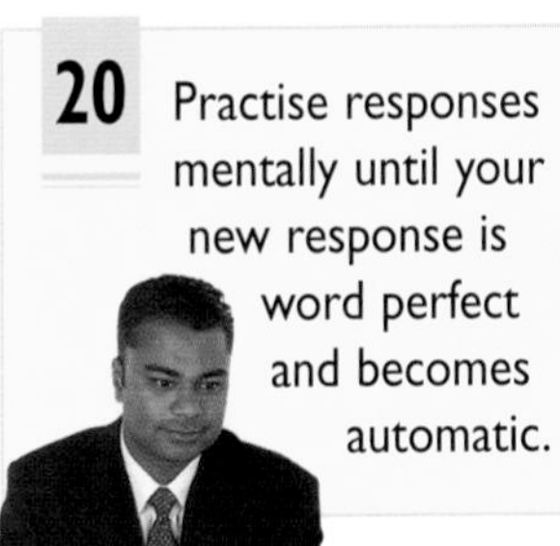

# MANAGING EMOTIONS

*Learn the skill of actively managing your emotional states, so that your working performance is maximized. Aim to manage your emotional states well at work and you will begin to thrive on challenging and potentially stressful situations.*

**21** Remember you can change the way you react to situations.

### POINTS TO REMEMBER

- If you allow situations to affect you emotionally, your working performance will suffer.
- Sometimes the key skill is to be aware of your own emotional state.
- It is possible to choose a different emotional state.
- Increasing your choice of emotion can transform your work.

## DEALING WITH STRESS

When you get stressed, your emotional state deteriorates, affecting your thinking, judgment, and performance. For example, when you "have to" deliver something important but "cannot" because of other commitments, your mind may perceive a "dangerous" situation. This can create anxiety and poor thinking. To cope with stressful situations, you can either change your perception of the situation until it becomes a positive challenge, or, you can change your emotional state to deal with it better.

## ACHIEVING "FLOW"

Top performers spend most of their time in a state of "flow" – a buzz you get from an activity you enjoy doing. This occurs when a goal is motivating and a challenge is appropriate to your level of skill. Aim to achieve this state more often. If you are bored, raise the level of challenge. If you are stressed, raise your level of competence, or increase the support you receive from others. Change your emotional state until you view a task as a chance to extend your abilities. It can help to break the task into smaller pieces to help you achieve "flow". Be aware of the state of flow of yourself and others.

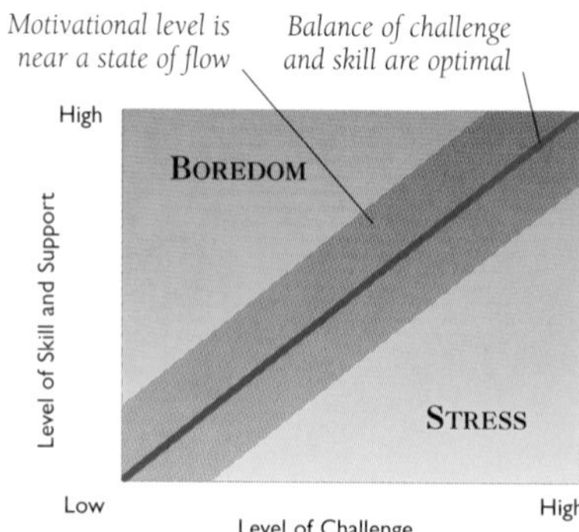


▲ **FINDING THE STATE OF FLOW**
*People are motivated when their levels of skill and support are equal to a challenge. A highly skilled person can become bored without a challenge and, conversely, too great a challenge can result in stress.*

## BECOMING AWARE

People are often unaware of their emotional states. There are hundreds of emotions you may go through in a day, such as frustration, anger, excitement, satisfaction, or relief. Once you recognize significant emotional states, treat them as signals to draw your attention to something you may have otherwise missed. For example, frustration with a project can alert you to problems that need your attention or direct you to a more useful emotional state, such as patience, because you know you have done what you can.

**22** Identify your own emotional states frequently.

**23** Make decisions only when you are feeling positive.

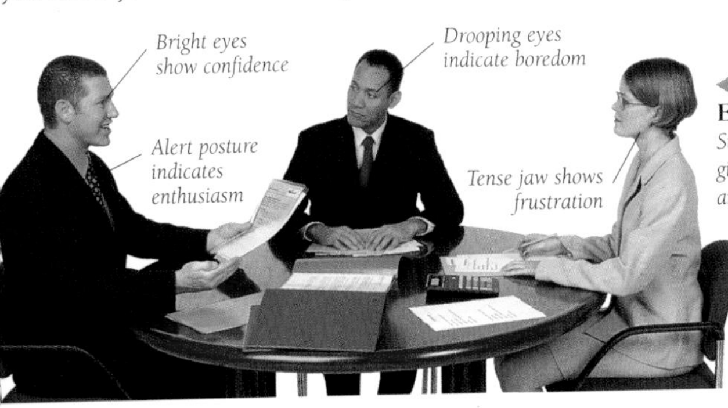
Bright eyes show confidence
Drooping eyes indicate boredom
Alert posture indicates enthusiasm
Tense jaw shows frustration

◀ **CALIBRATING EMOTIONS**
*Subtle physical signs can give you clues to positive and negative emotional states. Learn to spot these small cues in yourself and others, so that you know when to intervene.*

## ANCHORING EMOTIONS

Instead of feeling stressed, learn to create a positive emotional state. Think of a time when you experienced a positive state, such as feeling calm. Imagine you are back in that state. Look at what was happening around you then and notice how this makes you feel now. It is possible to access this feeling in future by connecting it to a trigger, or "anchor". Squeeze the tip of your thumb and a finger together in a specific way as the feeling builds and let go before the emotion peaks. Repeat this procedure so that you build an automatic response.

Squeezes thumb and finger to trigger an emotion

▲ **TRIGGERING EMOTIONS**
*Use a gesture as a link, or an anchor, to a positive state that you can trigger whenever you begin to feel stressed.*

# COACHING YOURSELF

*Most of us have learnt to become our own worst critics. Change the way you talk within yourself so that you can turn this inner critic into an inner coach, and learn to use the three-step self-coaching process for ongoing personal development.*

**24** Improve your self-talk so that you can boost your performance.

**25** Make sure you give yourself frequent encouragement.

**26** Notice when your internal dialogue starts becoming unhelpful.

## ENCOURAGING YOURSELF

Your inner dialogue will often determine your thoughts and feelings, and self-talk can often be negative. For example, when something you do goes wrong, you may say to yourself, "Why do I keep getting things wrong?" This dialogue may keep replaying a negative scene and make you feel bad about yourself. If you catch yourself doing this, replace negativity with more positive self-talk. Focus on a positive aspect, however minor. Say things like, "No-one is perfect. You are still learning".

▼ **NOTICING EFFECTS OF POSITIVE AND NEGATIVE SELF-TALK**

*Recognize the different physical responses you have when you talk to yourself. Ask yourself positive and negative questions, and notice how you respond physically and emotionally.*

Upright posture indicates confidence
Facial expression is relaxed

POSITIVE INNER DIALOGUE

Hunched shoulders indicate worry
Facial muscles are tense

NEGATIVE INNER DIALOGUE

### QUESTIONS TO ASK YOURSELF

**Q** What do I need to do differently?

**Q** Am I running any negative self-talk instead of being positive about myself?

**Q** What is the most useful way to coach myself through this one?

**Q** What assumptions am I making that could be worth looking at again?

**27** Look on the bright side, rather than always expecting the worst.

# INNER COACHING VOICE

The voice that you talk to yourself with is made up of three main components: speed, tone, and volume. Alter any one of these factors if you want to change the way you feel. For example, if you feel unmotivated, speed up your inner voice and turn up the volume to increase your motivation. Try using the voice tones of whoever is best at motivating you. If you are feeling emotionally low from a work encounter, slow your inner voice down, turn down the volume, and use a caring tone so you can reach a more positive state.

### DOS AND DON'TS

- ✔ Do remember that self-talk affects your behaviour.
- ✔ Do notice which self-talk works best.
- ✔ Do use humour in your self-talk.
- ✘ Don't ignore your inner dialogue.
- ✘ Don't dwell on negative thoughts about others.
- ✘ Don't be hard on yourself over an issue.

# USING SELF-COACHING

You can resolve many difficulties by using the three-stage self-coaching model – problem, outcome, and action. First, identify a problem: for example, when a colleague threatens sales by neglecting a task. Second, check that you are clear on the outcome you want. You may decide to motivate the person rather than get somebody else to complete the task. Third, identify what you would do differently. Ask yourself, "What is the best way to motivate them?" Decide on the best approach and imagine yourself doing it.

**28** Ensure you are comfortable with an approach before you carry it out.

▼ **COACHING YOURSELF**

*Focus on developing positive self-talk habits through self-coaching, and benefit from the improvement in your confidence levels.*

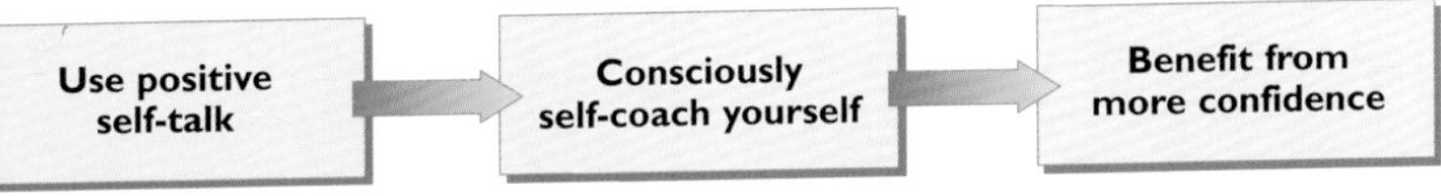
Use positive self-talk
Consciously self-coach yourself
Benefit from more confidence

# VISUALIZING FOR EFFECTIVENESS

*Visual thinking is a major tool in effective management, helping in meetings, negotiations, and problem solving. Optimize your visual thinking for mental rehearsal and creative management so that you can achieve more with less effort.*

**29** Practise visualizing regularly so that you become better at it.

### MAKING DECISIONS

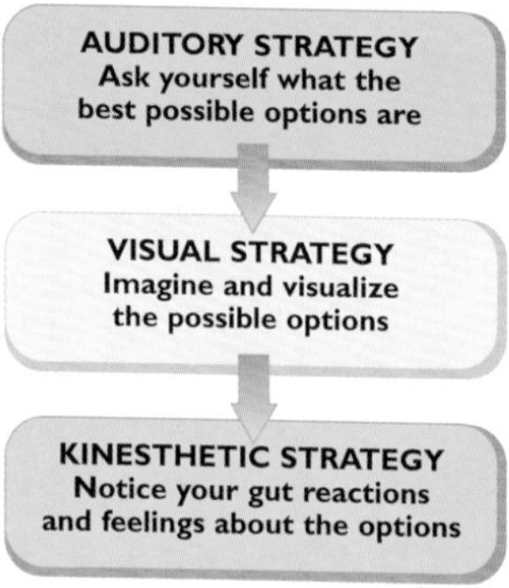

**AUDITORY STRATEGY**
**Ask yourself what the best possible options are**

**VISUAL STRATEGY**
**Imagine and visualize the possible options**

**KINESTHETIC STRATEGY**
**Notice your gut reactions and feelings about the options**

## YOUR VISUAL BRAIN

The three main languages of the brain are auditory, visual, and kinesthetic (feelings). These modes of thinking have different strengths and weaknesses. Increase your effectiveness by having the three modes working together, each in their strength areas. Visual thinking is best for imagining a lot of possibilities very quickly. This will work only when your visual thinking is driven by your inner dialogue (auditory internal dialogue) asking quality questions. Your kinesthetic sense is good for deciding which options are best. Utilize these languages to help you make quality decisions.

USING ▶ VISUALIZATION

*In this case study, an account manager found that if she substituted unnecessary self-talk with a visualization technique, she could dramatically increase the speed of her thinking processes.*

CASE STUDY

An account manager, Julia, had problems with the amount of reports she needed to read in a short space of time. No matter how hard she tried, she could not speed up her reading, and this affected her performance. She approached a friend of hers who had trained as an NLP practitioner. In a single session, the practitioner discovered what the problem was and subsequently her reading speed started to improve. It turned out that Julia was saying the words to herself in her head as she read. This, of course, meant that the speed of reading was limited by the speed of speech. The practitioner showed her how to curl her tongue back to switch off this internal self-talk. At the same time, she learnt how to visualize the meaning of the words directly. This method is considerably quicker than the speed of speech.

## CHANGING THE MIND'S EYE

The way you visualize makes a difference to how you feel and the results you get. You can increase or reduce your feelings by making changes in how you visualize. Suppose you feel worried about a project. You realize that you have an overwhelming image of all the potential problems. Take an image of one problem at a time and make it smaller. Push it into the distance. Notice when the problem stops feeling overwhelming. Alternatively, when you want to feel more motivated to achieve a positive goal, make your image of the goal larger, closer, and more colourful. Notice when you feel more motivated.

**30** Practise visualizing events in a number of different ways.

**31** Change visual images so that you can change your emotional state.

## WORKING WITH YOUR VISUALIZATIONS

| VISUAL ELEMENT | FACTORS TO CONSIDER |
|---|---|
| SIZE | How large is the problem you are visualizing? Make the problem grow smaller by visualizing it reducing in size. |
| VIEWPOINT | Do you see yourself in the picture, or are you an observer? Imagine yourself taking positive control of the situation. |
| COLOUR | Are you thinking of the task in colour or in black and white? Motivate yourself by visualizing the task in bright, vivid colours. |
| MOTION | Is the image motionless or moving, and is it at normal speed? Slow down images when you reach critical issues. |
| DISTANCE | How far away is the image from you? Bring an image closer to make it more important. |
| PERSPECTIVE | Does the image have depth as it would appear in real life, or is it flat like a picture? Motivate yourself with full, 3-D images. |

# REHEARSING MENTALLY

The visual skill of mental rehearsal is crucial for maximizing performance. It helps you practise your part in critical situations, such as interviews, until you achieve a high standard. Imagine playing a video of yourself in an important situation. Notice the part you feel anxious about. Keep playing, looking at different ways of improving performance until you are satisfied with your results. Imagine the scene more realistically – step inside the image of yourself. Notice weaknesses in your performance and imagine improvements until you are satisfied.

### THINGS TO DO

1. Imagine how you could deal with any difficulties a new task presents.
2. Practise imagining different responses to the situation.
3. Choose the best solution from your various options.

**32** Imagine various ways you could respond to a difficult situation, so that you are prepared beforehand.

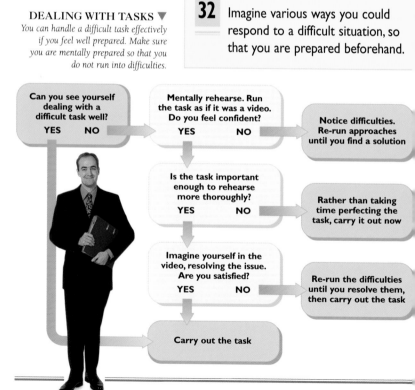

### DEALING WITH TASKS ▼

*You can handle a difficult task effectively if you feel well prepared. Make sure you are mentally prepared so that you do not run into difficulties.*

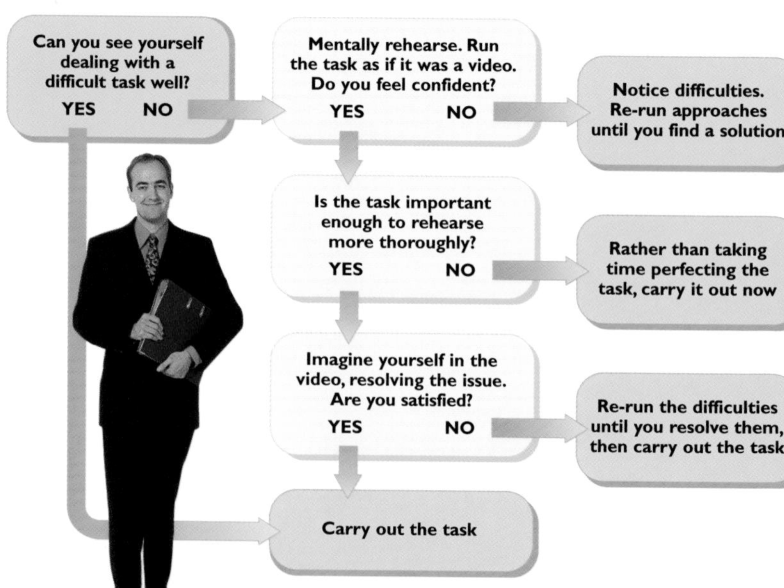

Can you see yourself dealing with a difficult task well?
YES NO
Mentally rehearse. Run the task as if it was a video. Do you feel confident?
YES NO
Notice difficulties. Re-run approaches until you find a solution
Is the task important enough to rehearse more thoroughly?
YES NO
Rather than taking time perfecting the task, carry it out now
Imagine yourself in the video, resolving the issue. Are you satisfied?
YES NO
Re-run the difficulties until you resolve them, then carry out the task
Carry out the task

## REHEARSING REALISTICALLY

Your mind stores images in two different ways so that you can differentiate between reality and imagination. First, think of something you did today, then imagine something you could have done instead. Notice how the real images are different from the imagined ones in terms of their size, colour, brightness, and clarity. Now, pretend your imagined event is real. The images will probably become big, bright, and moving. Aim to rehearse in the way your mind thinks of real events.

**33** Avoid imagining situations in the form of daydreams.

**34** Build personal flexibility by rehearsing options.

### QUESTIONS TO ASK YOURSELF

**Q** What is crucial to my overall performance now?

**Q** Would it benefit me to rehearse this?

**Q** Can my unconscious mind start rehearsing this?

**Q** Has my mind learnt to rehearse automatically?

## KNOWING WHEN TO REHEARSE

Some events are crucial to your overall performance, whereas others may not be. Regularly ask yourself which events are strategically most important to achieving your objectives. This tells you when to spend time on mental rehearsal. When something is critical, you usually have a growing feeling of anxiety or excitement. Focus on spotting these first signs, and then rehearse.

## CREATING YOUR RESOURCE ROOM

Expand your visual capabilities further by developing the visual-thinking skills that complement mental rehearsal. First, visualize your ideal setting. It may be by the sea, or in a spaceship. Think what you would want in this ideal "resource room". This may include a library of books; a comfortable chair and viewing screen; a device that improves emotional state; a way to materialize any mentor of your choosing. Go to this imaginary room when you need to think things through.

▲ **FORMING A RESOURCE ROOM**
*Whenever you have a creative task to do and need some inspiration, picture yourself in your ideal setting and tap into your internal creativity.*

# FINDING THE BEST APPROACH

*Turning around difficult situations using a positive approach, or "frame", allows you to keep yourself and others more motivated. Learn to be more positive at work – your satisfaction level will increase and the productivity of your team will rise.*

**35** Be aware of your negative approaches and change them.

**36** Change resentment towards work to an appreciation of self-development opportunities.

## FINDING POSITIVE FRAMES

Remember that events only have the meaning you give them. For example, do you see a glass of water as being half-full or half-empty? Your response tells you a lot about the way you "frame" situations. The same goes for your attitude to work. You may either look at work as a never-ending succession of problems, or as a string of exciting and challenging opportunities. Maintain your positive attitude in any situation and your satisfaction with your working life will improve.

### REFRAMING SITUATIONS

Treat negative thoughts in yourself or others as opportunities to think about things in a more useful way. For example, an employee may say that every time a working procedure is changed, he or she becomes confused. Reframe this problem by making constructive points:

*"It is good that you have noticed you get confused, because now we can clarify the procedures."*

*"You may be confused now, but it will all become clear when you have learnt the new skills."*

*"If we understand what is causing the confusion, we can look at how to present changes differently."*

*"Your confusion is evidence that you are learning something new and changing your normal routine."*

# PREPARING FOR PROBLEMS

A good way of carefully phrasing statements so that you elicit the best response is preframing. Anticipate an employee's response to an issue and guess their main objection. Then consider the best approach to the subject in view of their objection, and imagine yourself dealing with it in this way. For example, you are about to give somebody some extra work. You guess their main issue will be not having time to plan effectively. "Preframe" the extra work by saying, "Some extra work has come in and, fortunately, we have enough time to reorganize."

**37** Decide on the most useful and constructive ways to approach different situations.

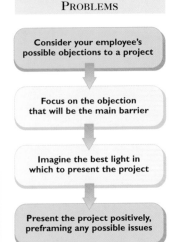

## PREFRAMING PROBLEMS

**Consider your employee's possible objections to a project**

↓

**Focus on the objection that will be the main barrier**

↓

**Imagine the best light in which to present the project**

↓

**Present the project positively, preframing any possible issues**

*Manager reminds employee of a specific project and presents it with a positive approach*

*Has papers ready to refer to if there are any queries*

*Employee reacts positively to manager's approach*

▼ **THINKING ABOUT CONTEXT**

*When you approach an employee with a new task, outline the context before giving the detail. Try to anticipate their reaction and preframe any possible problem issues in a positive light.*

# FREEING UP YOUR INNER RESOURCES

*Inner conflict saps energy and motivation. If you can identify and resolve conflicts, you can free up time and effort that would otherwise be wasted. Work to resolve inner conflicts so that you are not fighting against yourself and wasting your own energy.*

**38** Resolve any doubts you have before you commit to an action.

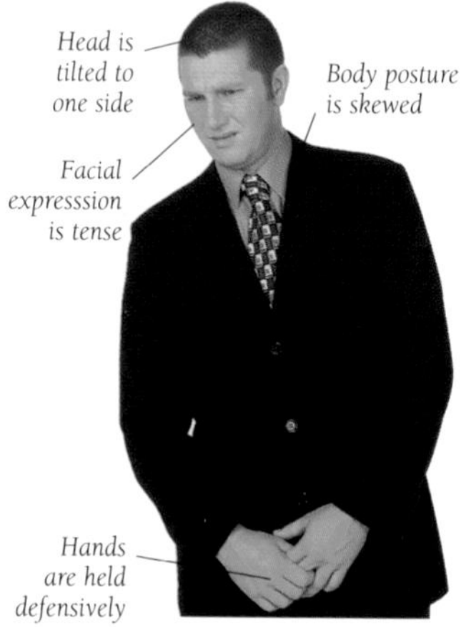
Head is tilted to one side
Body posture is skewed
Facial expresssion is tense
Hands are held defensively

▲ **RECOGNIZING YOUR PHYSICAL UNCERTAINTY**
*There are mental and physical signs of doubt. Recognize signs of your physical uncertainty, so that you can act on them.*

**39** Watch yourself on video and look for signs of uncertainty.

## RECOGNIZING INNER CONFLICT

There are many types of internal conflict that are relatively common and easy to spot, such as your own interests versus those of your colleagues, or professional demands on your time versus family demands. Internal conflict often shows up as mixed feelings. For example, when someone puts pressure on you to do something, you hear yourself saying "Yes" while noticing a small, uncomfortable feeling. Realize that this feeling shows you that you have an inner conflict. Pinpoint these feelings so that you can start to resolve any conflicting issues.

### QUESTIONS TO ASK YOURSELF

**Q** Do I recognize subtle feelings of doubt in myself?

**Q** When I notice I have doubts, do I act to resolve the underlying issues?

**Q** How do my feelings of doubt differ from my feelings of certainty?

**Q** What do I feel when I am certain about an issue?

**Q** Have I identified any work issues I routinely have doubts about?

**Q** Do I see how these feelings of doubt can be used to make positive changes?

### POINTS TO REMEMBER

- Top performers know how to get the best out of themselves by using their unconscious minds to resolve difficult issues.
- Poor performers massively underuse the potential of their unconscious.
- Most of our inner resources are unconscious.

**40** Make a list of any conflicting interests at work.

## RESOLVING ISSUES UNCONSCIOUSLY

You may often find that problems get resolved after a good night's sleep. This is because your unconscious mind works on problems while you are asleep. Use the potential of your unconscious mind. When you cannot resolve a problem, turn it into a question for your unconscious mind to think about. For instance, an employee may be underperforming and you are unsure what to do. Ask your unconscious, "Come up with some options. Let me know when you have got the best?"

TIME

MONEY

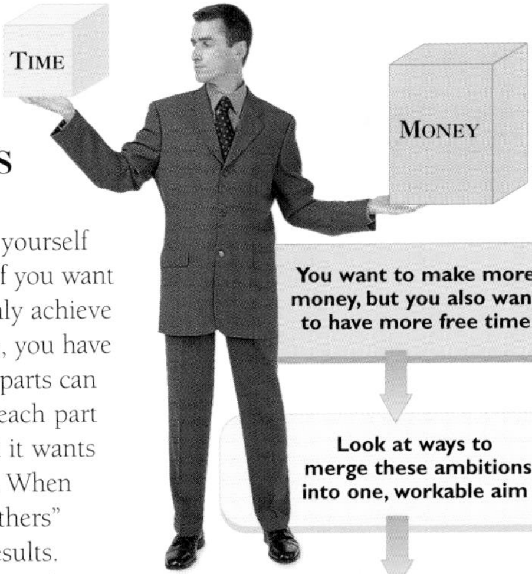

**You want to make more money, but you also want to have more free time**

**Look at ways to merge these ambitions into one, workable aim**

**Imagine a future "you" who is focused on the positive intentions of both ambitions**

**You will start to have ideas to help you achieve more money and more free time**

## RESOLVING ISSUES CONSCIOUSLY

A conflict implies two aspects of yourself fighting each other. For example, if you want career success but feel you can only achieve this at the expense of other people, you have a conflict. Think about how these parts can work together and imagine what each part wants. Ask the "success" part what it wants – you realize it wants recognition. When you think about the "expense of others" part, you realize it wants better results. Think about how they can work together. Imagine a future "you" that can improve both results and recognition. Recognize that you can achieve both by spending time supporting others.

SEEING POSSIBILITIES ▶

*Visualize two seemingly contradictory possibilities you want to work towards. Imagine the future resolution of the conflict by spending time looking at the positive intentions behind each "part". Think how each part could help the other achieve mutual aims.*

# LEARNING TO BREAK BAD HABITS

*Bad habits can prevent you from getting things done with ease, but it is relatively easy to change a habit by replacing an old behaviour with a more productive, new one. Remember that this is one of the easiest ways to continuously improve performance.*

**41** Know how to spot and change habits that limit your effectiveness.

**42** Understand that being aware of bad habits is the first step towards changing them.

## UNDERSTANDING HABITS

Habits are ways of automating a bundle of thought and behaviour sequences. For instance, when you think to yourself "collect e-mail", you press all the computer keys automatically, without conscious effort. Unfortunately, your brain is as good at running bad habits as useful ones. Realize that if you continue to think the way you have always thought, you will continue to get what you have always got. If a bad habit is automatic, it will keep occurring because it is outside conscious awareness.

## RECOGNIZING HABITS

Blind spots about your limitations can limit your professional development. Be willing to admit your own weaknesses so you can look objectively at your own bad habits. Watch out for some of the most common habits that hinder you from achieving the highest standards. Notice yourself using these habits so that you will know what to change for the better. Extend your concept of positive habits to include any thoughts or behaviours that will boost your effectiveness. Remember, nearly everything you do, whether thought or behaviour, becomes habitual once you have repeated it a few times.

### POINTS TO REMEMBER

- Remember that the level of your performance is related to the effectiveness of your habits.
- People's personalities consist of the habits that they keep running over and over again.
- Generally, people change their habits when an alternative seems more appealing.
- Your habits need to change when you are no longer getting the results you want.

## EXAMINING GOOD AND BAD HABITS

| HABITS WORTH LOSING | HABITS WORTH HAVING |
|---|---|
| **EXPERIENCING STRESS** Feeling pressured causes stress and anxiety. | **FEELING IN CONTROL** Focusing on your strengths is empowering. |
| **PROCRASTINATING** Wasting time is inefficient and saps motivation. | **SETTING DAILY GOALS** Working towards set goals is motivating. |
| **SELF-CRITICIZING** Being hard on yourself undermines confidence. | **EXPECTING THE BEST** Having high standards results in good returns. |
| **BEING A VICTIM** Not being assertive lowers your potential. | **REMAINING PERSISTENT** Being determined increases your confidence. |

### USING THE "SWISH PATTERN"

**Identify and focus on a bad habit you want to change. Visualize it**

↓

**Imagine your ideal self in the future having broken the habit. Visualize the new, ideal habit**

↓

**Replace the first image with the second, then look away. Repeat 5 times**

↓

**Recall the first picture and check that it now starts to change itself automatically**

## CHANGING HABITS

Once you have spotted a habit you want to change, such as getting frustrated with a colleague, use the NLP "Swish" pattern to change it. Re-run the experience of being frustrated. Identify what you see when you begin to become frustrated. Magnify this image. Now, give your mind something more useful to aim at. Imagine an ideal image of yourself in the future having handled the issue well. Expand this image over the original one. Shift your attention elsewhere. Now repeat this process five times until the second image replaces the first automatically. Do this regularly until the new habit is automatically triggered whenever the old habit tries to run.

**43** Remember that all top performers have spent years building the habits of success.

# ANALYZING PROBLEMS

*Problems are often seen from a limited perspective, whereas the answer may lie outside the "box", or problem space, in which you are thinking. Increase the size of your thinking box, so that you can get to solutions you would not otherwise reach.*

**44** Identify the level at which a problem needs to be addressed.

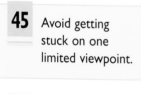

**45** Avoid getting stuck on one limited viewpoint.

**46** View problems as puzzles that you need to work on to solve.

## EXPLORING LEVELS

Managers often get stuck by tackling problems at the wrong level. When you are exploring a problem, make sure you consider the six possible levels. When you personalize your desk, for example, you are making an environmental level change. Saying "thank you" to people more often is a behavioural change. Going for higher targets is a change in the level of expectation. Developing a new skill is a change in capability. Promotion can bring about change at an identity level. Shifting focus from the bottom line to staff development represents a change at the level of values.

## EXPLORING VIEWPOINTS

Once you have explored the level of a problem, think through all the viewpoints involved, including those of your colleagues, customers, and business. Understand the viewpoints so that you can find the best solution for all. Whenever there is a problem, ensure you can describe it equally well from each party's viewpoint. If you are not sure, ask them. Suppose a customer does not care about cost, only about delivery deadlines. To keep costs down, the business uses postal delivery. However, you are worried that the material will not arrive on time. Ask the customer if they would rather pay for a special delivery. This could satisfy all parties.

### QUESTIONS TO ASK YOURSELF

**Q** How can I think about this problem in a different way so that I can come to a solution?

**Q** What is the most useful and productive way to think about this?

**Q** Does this problem exist only in my head?

**Q** When is the best time to think about this problem?

**Q** Is there an angle that I have not yet examined?

## ASSESSING THE DIFFERENT ASPECTS OF AN ISSUE

| FACTOR | ASPECT | POSSIBLE SOLUTION |
|---|---|---|
| LEVEL | VALUES | If a different meaning and purpose were perceived, could this transform the situation? |
| | IDENTITY | Could a change in someone's self-perception be the key to solving the problem? |
| | CAPABILITY | Is learning a new skill the best way forward in this situation? |
| | EXPECTATION | If someone had a different assumption, could this make the difference? |
| | BEHAVIOUR | Would one difference in what somebody does be the answer? |
| | ENVIRONMENT | Can a simple change in where something happens solve the problem? |
| TIMESCALE | PAST | What personal resource from the past would be most effective in resolving this issue? |
| | PRESENT | What is the smallest thing that could be done right now to make a start on this issue? |
| | FUTURE | What solution becomes obvious when you imagine a future where the problem is solved? |
| VIEWPOINT | SELF | Is there something you need to do differently for this not to be a problem? |
| | OTHER | Does someone else need to do something differently in order to solve this problem? |
| | OBSERVER | What solution is obvious only from an outside point of view? |

# OPTIMIZING YOUR TIME

*The way you spend your time will determine your overall performance, and this in turn will have an effect on your team. Couple time-management skills with what really motivates you, and you will immediately start to boost your results.*

**47** Make sure you spend some time every day focusing on priorities.

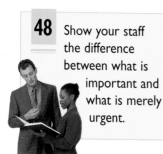

**48** Show your staff the difference between what is important and what is merely urgent.

## KNOWING THE BASICS

The key to success at work is knowing the difference between what is important and what is just urgent. For instance, developing your management skills is important, but it is too often squeezed out by the pressure of urgent, but less vital, matters. Reallocate your time to important issues. Ask yourself, "Is this the most useful thing I could be doing now?" Focus on tasks that are important to you, and you will be better motivated.

## PRIORITIZING IMPORTANT TASKS OVER URGENT TASKS

URGENT / IMPORTANT
If you spend time stressed and in crisis management, these are symptoms that you are allowing urgent tasks to dominate important tasks.

IMPORTANT / NOT URGENT
If you take the time to plan your goals and development, you are using your time well and allocating time to important tasks.

URGENT / NOT IMPORTANT
If you are interrupted by office gossip and personal calls, you are not prioritizing your time to matters that are important.

NOT IMPORTANT / NOT URGENT
If you waste time reading junk mail, you are spending time that you could better spend on important tasks.

### POINTS TO REMEMBER

- You should maintain a good emotional state so that you remain motivated.
- If you have trouble with time management, set up a coaching session so that you can work on making improvements.
- Time management is the only activity you can spend time doing that will give you more time.

**MANAGING YOUR TIME ▼**
*Begin by refocusing on your core values. Review them, and then reprioritize your work to align with these values.*

## ASSESSING VALUES

One reason you may not be practising time management is because you are losing sight of the personal reasons for doing what you are doing. You are unable to see the wood for the trees. Refocus on your core values to help motivate yourself. Do this by asking yourself, "What is important about work?" Then, free-associate by writing down the different thoughts that come into your head. This will surface your work values. Common motivating values include satisfaction, career success, recognition, helping others, and financial rewards. Once you have ten or more, rank your top three core values.

**Refocus** → **Review** → **Reprioritize**

## MOTIVATING YOURSELF

If you tend to think of time management as being either a boring chore or something that reminds you of everything you have been putting off, then you will never do it. If, on the other hand, you begin to think of time management as the shortest route to achieving more of what you really want, it becomes compelling. Avoid work overload by breaking your time into smaller tasks and get into the habit of doing this on a daily basis. It is easier to enjoy accomplishing one task at a time, and it is motivating and satisfying as you tick off each task on the list.

**▲ MANAGING YOUR TIME**
*To avoid overload, break your work into bite-size chunks that are as easy and as satisfying to do as possible. The tasks inevitably feel more achievable and you will feel motivated to tackle them.*

**49** Learn to understand what matters to you so that you are better motivated in your work.

# HELPING OTHERS IMPROVE

Increasingly, the competitive edge in an organization depends upon people's interpersonal skills. Use NLP skills to help you get the best from other people.

## RELATING NON-VERBALLY

*Most business results are generated through good working relationships between people. Understand and adopt the basic principles and skills of non-verbal communication, so that you can enhance your working relationships.*

**50** Learn to see your behaviour from other people's perspectives.

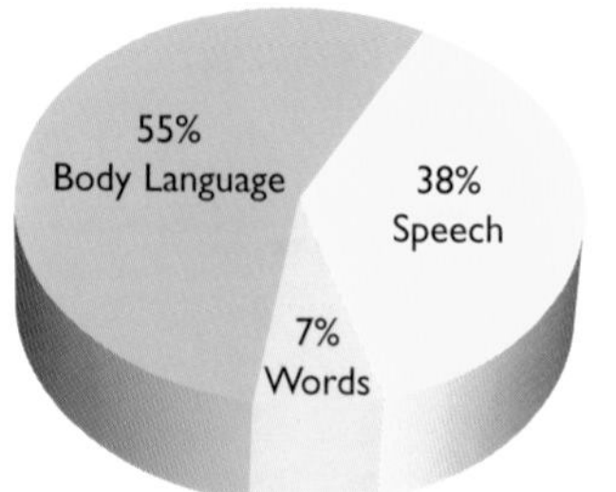


▲ **IMPACT OF COMMUNICATION**
*Research shows that, in face-to-face communication, voice tones and body language have a far greater effect in terms of how people react and respond to each other than words themselves.*

### GETTING ON BETTER

Working relationships are like a dance. If you alter your behaviour, other people change theirs accordingly. To be an outstanding manager, learn to practise essential attitudes. Assume people are doing the best they can from their point of view. Believe improvements will come if you work out what you can do differently to get the best out of your staff. Support them and spell out clearly what they need to do to succeed, and then make it possible for them to do it.

## PACING AND LEADING

When you communicate, it is important to acknowledge what is being said in some way. "Pacing" can be done non-verbally, by nodding your head in response to a point, or verbally, by summarizing each point made. The person you are talking with then feels confident that you are listening to what he or she is saying and will be more receptive as you "lead" with a question or comment. This helps you redirect the flow to the next most useful place.

# MATCHING BEHAVIOURS

When people have a rapport, they tend to match each other's body language and voice tone. Tune in your body language and voice to other people's preferred styles. Notice the way people express themselves and shift your style so that it is similar. Listen to voice tones and notice when someone speaks faster or quieter. Speed up or alter your volume accordingly. If someone makes a lot of fast gestures, speed up and increase your gestures to help increase rapport.

Matches voice tone
Has calm voice tone
Sits in matching position
Feet are crossed

**ADAPTING STYLES** ▶
*In this example, the manager has adapted her body language and voice tone to match the employee's. Her behaviour affects the response she receives from the employee and helps create a rapport.*

# AVOIDING MISMATCHING

Beware of sending powerful negative messages non-verbally, such as by frowning when someone suggests an idea. This "mismatching" can damage relationships and performance. Even though you may not intend to give this signal, your unconscious communication affects the response that you will get. For instance, if you do not look up when someone talks to you, you may be sending a dismissive signal. Prevent this by becoming aware of your own unconscious mismatching and increase the quality of attention you give to others.

**51** Remember, it is not what you say, but how you say it.

**52** Aim to always bring out the best in others.

# EVALUATING PRIORITIES

*In every aspect of business, such as in customer service, staff retention, and performance management, people have priorities that need to be satisfied. Learn how to identify key needs, so that you are in a position to be able to satisfy them.*

**53** Practise listening for people's personal criteria in all situations.

**54** Focus on issues that directly affect performance.

**55** Keep a written note of customers' main priorities.

## UNDERSTANDING CRITERIA

One cause of failure in business stems from staff not being clear about the needs they are trying to fulfil. Develop the habit of automatically identifying the criteria that has the most affect on your results (key performance criteria) to ensure that you and your team focus attention on the most productive issues. For example, realize that it is more cost effective to retain existing customers than to win new ones. In your own organization, encourage your staff to become more aware of customers' priorities.

## NOTICING EMPHASIS

Listen for other people's most important criteria, or ask them what they consider to be important. Sometimes their words alone will tell you. Notice the way they "mark" out their key criteria among a flow of apparent needs. They may say, "We need you to get back to us soon". The key word "soon" may be marked out with a verbal emphasis or a hand gesture. Identify the key criteria and check it by repeating it back.

Hand gesture emphasizes point
A raised voice tone underlines an important issue

**EMPHASIZING A POINT ▶**
*What someone else considers as important may be different from your view. Watch the way people show what they consider relevant through their gestures and voice.*

## CLARIFYING OTHER PEOPLE'S NEEDS

When you are responsible for delivering results to others, clarify their main criteria. NLP skills will help you identify and satisfy needs. Ask, "If we can deliver X at this price by next week, is that what you want?" If there are no problems, agree to line up the next action steps. If there are problems, ask questions to find out what is going to cause the difficulty for you or them. Then discuss it to find the best way forward for both of you.

### POINTS TO REMEMBER

- You will retain more staff if you identify their key needs.
- You can improve relationships with customers by asking them what is important to them.
- In any situation, keep thinking about what is important in order to remain focused.
- Taking the time to clarify criteria will save time in the long-term.

*Colleague listens to points of view*

*Manager asks what is important about an issue*

*Employee leans forward to make his point*

## CLARIFYING INTERNAL NEEDS

When you rely on your team to be responsible for delivering results, first be sure that you have made the performance criteria clear. For example, there is little point in asking people to improve quality if you have not said which aspects of quality need improving, and to what standard. Firstly, ask your team if they are clear about what is wanted. If you are not convinced they are clear, ask them to repeat back what is wanted. Secondly, make sure they are able to deliver what you want.

▲ **LISTENING TO VIEWPOINTS**

*Take the time to ask your team members about their priorities on a project, so that they feel respected, and so that you can ensure that everyone is clear on the goals.*

**56** Keep clarifying to your team what is important in each situation.

# WORKING WITH PERSONALITY TRAITS

*In most situations, there are some ways in which people will behave consistently. Recognize these consistent patterns in yourself and others, so you increase your effectiveness and ensure you avoid the same problems repeating themselves over and over again.*

**57** Prevent problems by understanding your colleagues' behaviour patterns.

**58** Learn to recognize patterns in yourself, as well as in others.

**59** See how every mental habit can be a strength.

## LOOKING AT DIFFERENCES

There are mental habits (or "meta-programs") that we all use in different situations. For example, some people follow a set procedure to achieve their goals, and others prefer to have options. Evaluations can be based on people's own opinions, or on those of others. Some people initiate action, while others are reactive. Some aim to achieve positive goals, and others want to avoid negative problems. Some people think in overview, and others focus on fine details. People may also look for how things are similar to, or different from, each other.

## ADAPTING TO DIFFERENCE

Two people with different meta-programs can find it hard to communicate, and this can be damaging in business. Learn to recognize different patterns of behaviour in your team members, and work with these differences to maximize performance. For example, when you delegate a task to someone who favours "options" to achieve their aims, as opposed to a set procedure, avoid telling them exactly what to do. They are likely to feel you do not trust them. Tell them the goal and let them decide on the best way of achieving it.

### QUESTIONS TO ASK YOURSELF

**Q** When I delegate tasks to someone who favours procedures, do I make sure they know what to do?

**Q** Does this person focus on the positive or is he or she more focused on avoiding the negative?

**Q** Have I designed this job to suit this person's strengths?

## APPLYING DIFFERENCES

Try to differentiate between people with different personalities in your team. Improve performance by ensuring that people's characteristics fit their job specifications. For example, an account executive is likely to perform better if he or she is naturally proactive, whereas a telesales person will excel if she or he reacts well to customers. Human Resources specialists use "meta-program" profiles to clarify the characteristics of top performers to recruit the best candidates.

**60** Make sure people's natural personality preferences are well matched to the tasks that they perform.

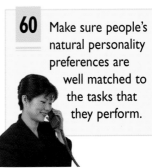

### WORKING WITH DIFFERENT PERSONALITY TRAITS

| META-PROGRAMS | EMPLOYEE DISCUSSION | MANAGER'S VIEW |
|---|---|---|
| PROACTIVE | "We just need to get this done." | "Good points. If *you* start on it right now, *you* can deal with issues that come up." |
| REACTIVE | "Let's wait until we know more." | |
| BIG PICTURE | "You are not seeing the overview." | "You are both right. With no overview, we will get lost and without fine detail, we fail." |
| FINE DETAIL | "The fine detail is just as important." | |
| PROCEDURE | "This is the way it is done here." | "If *you* keep things going, I would like *you* to consider the best options." |
| OPTION | "Yes, but we need fresh approaches." | |
| SELF | "I want to make the decision here." | "Maybe we need more details about the customer's wants before you make a decision." |
| OTHER | "Will the customer buy it?" | |
| TOWARDS | "I really want to meet this deadline." | "If *you* plan how to meet the deadline, *you* can make sure we do not repeat mistakes." |
| AWAY FROM | "We can't make another mistake." | |
| SIMILARITY | "We have had this problem before." | "Let's see what worked last time and tailor it to what is different." |
| DIFFERENCE | "The pace of change is different." | |

# GETTING THE BEST DEAL

*Not everyone has the same approach to negotiations – in fact, there are five main styles that people use unconsciously. Understand your own approach and learn to recognize other people's, so you get the best results for all parties in your negotiations.*

**61** Treat the other party's interests with the respect you give your own.

▲ **MAKING A DEAL**
*Find a way to work towards the best results through bargaining, so that all parties will be pleased with the result.*

## UNDERSTANDING STYLES

Learn to recognize negotiation styles in yourself and others. A compromise style splits the difference although both parties could have achieved more. A coercive style relies on being dominant regardless of consequences. Emotional negotiation assumes that appealing to feelings will get the best results, while rational negotiation supposes arguing a point of view will change people's minds. A bargaining style, however, is the most beneficial, because it finds the trade-offs that get the best value for all.

## RECOGNIZING NEGOTIATING STYLES

| NEGOTIATION STYLE | DISCUSSION |
|---|---|
| COMPROMISE | "We need a fair deal."<br>"Maybe we can agree to split the difference." |
| COERCION | "Can we negotiate that?"<br>"No, when we make demands, you should jump." |
| EMOTION | "Will you extend our credit terms?"<br>"That would cause difficulties for me." |
| RATIONAL | "Do you see that if we can agree now...?"<br>"But it is sensible to finalize the schedules first." |
| BARGAINING | "If you can deliver next week, we agree."<br>"We will deliver next week, if you sign the deal now." |

## DEVELOPING THE SKILLS

Recognize occasions that could be negotiation situations. Before a negotiation, be clear on your outcomes and your bottom line. Make sure you plan and research carefully beforehand, and think through what your best alternative to a negotiated agreement is. This might be to go elsewhere. During the negotiation, maintain a steady emotional state – if you find this difficult, take a deep breath and change the focus of your thinking. Every move should get you closer to a win-win deal or the realization that no deal is the best option.

### THINGS TO DO

1. Before a negotiation, try to imagine the other party's possible sticking points.
2. Gather any useful information on them.
3. Mentally rehearse the parts of the negotiation that you anticipate will be difficult.

**62** Know you are only as strong as your weakest moves.

**63** Work to achieve a good deal for both parties.

## BENEFITING THE BUSINESS

Expand your negotiating skills and reap the future rewards in your own performance. Remember that if a party is unhappy with the results of a deal, long-term relationships may be damaged. Review every negotiation with the benefit of hindsight and look at what you could do differently in future. Practise in your imagination and make it a goal to improve relationships with every deal. Also, take stakeholders into account with each negotiation, so that your business thrives in the long term. This is win-win-win thinking.

**NEGOTIATING SUCCESSFULLY ▶**

*In this example, a major organization used negotiation with their suppliers to position themselves as a market leader in environmentally friendly furniture. Excellence in negotiation allowed them to put together deals that their competition could not match.*

CASE STUDY

A leading furniture retailer decided to treat increasing concerns about the environment as an opportunity rather than a problem. Initially their suppliers were resistant to making environmentally friendly changes. The retailer negotiated improvements with each supplier in order to create alternative processes that reduced environmental damage. The suppliers in turn had to renegotiate with their supply chain. This was not an overnight process. Additionally, the retailer decided not to advertise this policy, but to let people hear of it through word of mouth. This method had higher credibility and saved on advertising. The policy was a win-win-win move as customers received sustainable quality products at good prices; the organization grew rapidly because of its reputation; and the environment benefited from reduced waste.

# DETECTING AND PREVENTING PROBLEMS

*It is best to avoid problems before they occur. Learn to anticipate them by recognizing subtle cues in other people's behaviour. Be sensitive and aim to spot other people's potential issues, even before they are aware of them themselves.*

**64** Recognize that every problem was once a solution to another problem.

**65** Remember, it is more cost efficient to prevent problems, rather than waiting until they happen.

## RECOGNIZING POTENTIAL PROBLEMS

Learn to spot problems in advance. Sometimes someone is aware of a problem, but it may not be at the front of their mind. This incongruence can affect their behaviour and can influence others. Begin to recognize signs of this and pick up on subtle signals. First, spot your own uncertainties, such as nagging doubts, and act on them. Second, notice mixed messages in others and ask questions so that you can detect a problem before it happens.

## KNOWING SELF-CERTAINTY

When you are about to make a decision, you need to have a way of recognizing your inner certainty. Unless you are certain, you could make a decision that you regret. Think of a time when you did have a feeling of certainty or inner congruence, and it turned out to be accurate. Focus on the inner feeling so that you could describe it in terms of size, shape, or location. Now compare this with a time when you were uncertain. Be aware of the differences between when you feel certain and when you do not. Then, check your certainty before you make a decision.

### QUESTIONS TO ASK YOURSELF

**Q** How certain is this person about what they are saying?

**Q** How sure am I about what I am saying?

**Q** What do I need to ask to clarify these feelings of doubt and uncertainty?

**Q** How will I know when this person is certain?

**Q** How congruent am I feeling about this decision?

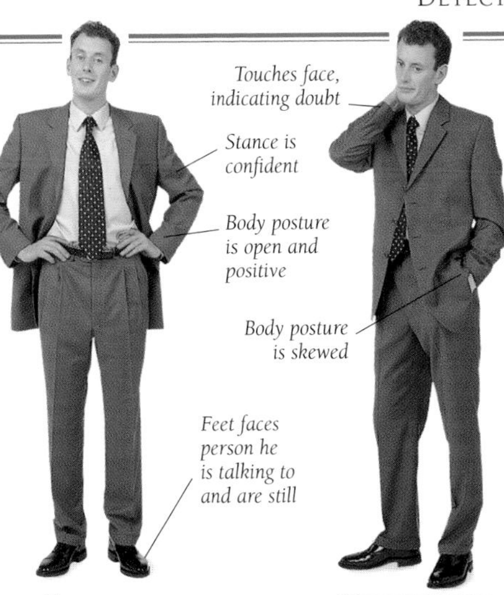
Touches face, indicating doubt
Stance is confident
Body posture is open and positive
Body posture is skewed
Feet faces person he is talking to and are still
CERTAINTY
UNCERTAINTY

▲ **MEASURING CERTAINTY**
*Listen and watch carefully when people respond and notice your gut feeling about their level of certainty. When someone is certain, their verbal and non-verbal behaviour say the same thing.*

## RESOLVING THE PROBLEM

Surface any hidden concerns, so you can find a way of resolving problems. Notice a concern and decide whether it is worth picking up on. If it is, say, "You don't seem to be clear about "X". If there was a problem with "X", what would it be?" Once the issue has surfaced, and if it seems to be significant, ask, "Do you know how to resolve that?" If they say "Yes", check for congruence. If they are incongruent, ask them again what the issue is. However, if they say "No", ask "What has to happen for us to resolve this?"

**CONVERSATIONAL CALIBRATION** ▶
*To measure congruence, ask a colleague two questions. First, ask a question that you know your colleague knows the answer to. Then ask one you know he or she is uncertain about. Notice the differences. Rate their congruence on a scale of 1–10.*

## FINDING DOUBT IN OTHERS

When someone is certain, their words make more sense, their voice tone tends to be deeper, and their body language more confident. When someone is uncertain, there will be a small element of doubt or hesitation in their behaviour – their body language is sending a message of uncertainty. Concerns will show up in subtle shifts in tone of voice, facial expression, skin coloration, or pupil dilation. Learn to watch for subtle incongruities of body language.

*Employee's voice tone and gestures are emphatic*

**RESPONDING WITH CONFIDENCE**

*Employee hesitates and looks away*

**RESPONDING WITH DOUBT**

# SHAPING MEETINGS

*By knowing how to make meetings work effectively, you can transform personal and organizational productivity. Improve your meetings skills so that meetings are always a constructive forum, where issues can be discussed efficiently and effectively.*

**66** Keep summarizing where the meeting has got to and where it is going.

## PREPARING MEETINGS

Ensure you are clear about the aim of a meeting. Ask yourself what you want to achieve by the end of the meeting. Break this into outcomes, such as decisions made and tasks allocated. Think about what you will see or hear to let you know that your goals have been achieved. For example, you will see people nod agreement to a decision; or you will hear someone offering to do a task. Finally, check that each person needs to be there for most of the items on the agenda, or schedule another meeting.

▼ **KEEPING A MEETING FOCUSED**

*Write down your meeting goals on a flipchart so that everyone present can refer to it if necessary, and watch for signs that outcomes are being achieved.*

### THINGS TO DO

1. Practise putting yourself in other people's positions so you can understand their viewpoint.
2. Work out the best way to move the meeting on.
3. Compliment others when they make a good point.

## TRACKING THE MEETING

Imagine watching the meeting from the corner of the room. Visualize yourself standing in a thoughtful pose in a position where you can observe the whole room. This is called 3rd position in NLP. Imagine moving into this position and notice if events are going anywhere. If they are, then continue as you were. If not, take charge and get agreement from everyone on the purpose of the meeting. Then, move into the 3rd position in your mind again. Keep checking that the meeting is progressing towards successful outcomes.

# KEEPING THE MEETING FOCUSED

Having started the meeting with the objectives in clear view of everyone, keep checking that the meeting is on track. If necessary, intervene. For example, if somebody is discussing something that is not directly relevant, say "Good point, but I am not sure how that is helping us achieve our aim, here" and refer everyone to the agenda. If things become unclear, summarize the goals you have already achieved and refocus on the next one. When you encounter problems, ask, "What can we do differently?" to move towards solutions. If you become stuck with someone, guess their problem in order to find a way forward.

**67** Summarize the goals achieved and refocus on the next one.

**68** Identify the next action steps and who will carry them out.

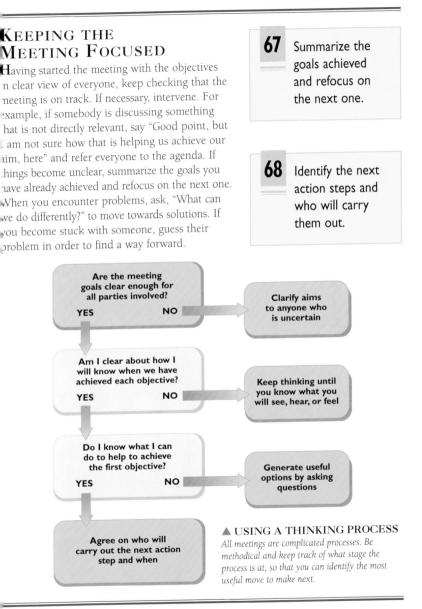

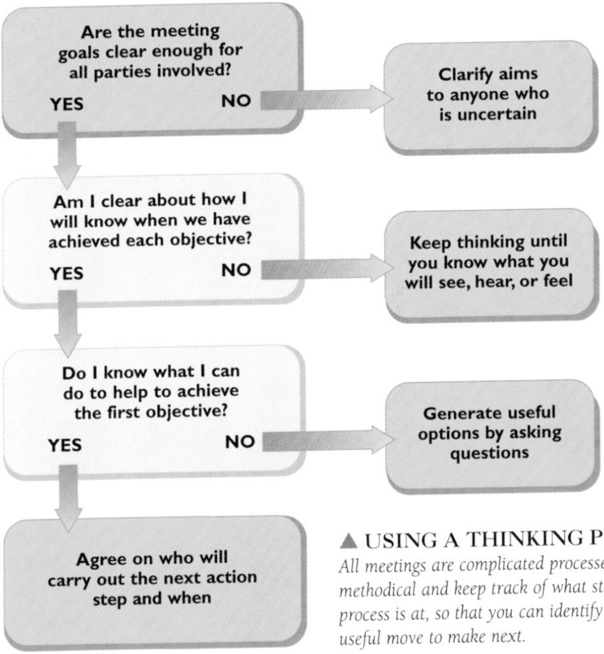

**Are the meeting goals clear enough for all parties involved?**
**YES** ↓ — **NO** → **Clarify aims to anyone who is uncertain**

**Am I clear about how I will know when we have achieved each objective?**
**YES** ↓ — **NO** → **Keep thinking until you know what you will see, hear, or feel**

**Do I know what I can do to help to achieve the first objective?**
**YES** ↓ — **NO** → **Generate useful options by asking questions**

**Agree on who will carry out the next action step and when**

▲ USING A THINKING PROCESS

*All meetings are complicated processes. Be methodical and keep track of what stage the process is at, so that you can identify the most useful move to make next.*

# IMPROVING WORKING RELATIONSHIPS

*Managers need high levels of interpersonal skills to achieve top performance in today's pressured working environment. Learn the vital skill of knowing when and how to shift viewpoints to ensure you get the best results from others.*

**69** Recognize the part you play in helping your staff deliver good results.

**70** Appreciate your employees' points of view.

**71** Notice whether people focus more on relationships or on tasks.

## LEARNING FROM WEAKNESSES

Successful managers need to achieve top results from their teams. To get the best out of people, look at what you do with people that works, and how to improve what does not work. When results are not up to standard, resist the urge to blame staff. Instead, notice your part in the results they produce. This could include things you did not do. Imagine alternative approaches that might work better next time. For example, a colleague does not seem to listen to your comments. On reflection, you realize that you told them only what you wanted, not how they should proceed.

### CULTURAL DIFFERENCES

The differences between individuals are much bigger than the differences between genders. However, there are some interesting stereotypical differences between men and women. Women are often better at putting themselves into other people's shoes (known as 2nd position in NLP). Conversely, they can neglect their own needs (in 1st position). Men on the other hand are often clearer about their own needs and more assertive in satisfying them. They can, however, be weak at understanding a viewpoint that is different to their own.

# MOVING YOUR VIEWPOINT

People often talk about the "real world" and forget hat each of us lives in our own world. Learn to ;ee situations from other people's viewpoints hrough "2nd positioning". Your own point of 'iew is "1st position". Also, try to be an impartial )bserver (3rd position) and view a situation 'rom outside any individual viewpoint. Use this )erceptual position to be objective. When you are 'aced with a difficulty, explore all three positions.

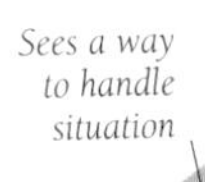

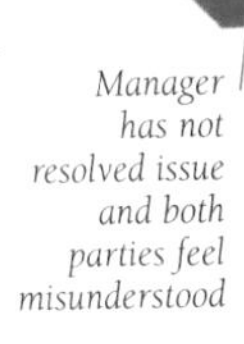

Manager confronts an employee about a problem on a project
Manager has not considered other perspectives
Communication breaks down
Manager has not resolved issue and both parties feel misunderstood
Thinks through situation from an observer's point of view
Sees a way to handle situation
Issue is resolved amicably

▲ **VALUING VIEWPOINTS**

*This manager must appreciate his employee's point of view from an observer position, so that he can constructively handle the situation.*

# DEALING WITH PROBLEMS

Imagine a situation with a colleague who you find lifficult. Choose a word to describe how you :xperience the colleague's behaviour as difficult, 'or example, hostile. Think how they may see your behaviour as difficult. Choose another word .o describe your behaviour. Imagine yourself in the ;ituation (1st position) and note how you feel. You nay be more frustrated than you realized. Focus )n the person's body language and imagine being n their position (2nd position). Notice any feeling hey might have that you were not aware of, such ıs anxiety. Then, step back (3rd position) and ask yourself, "What's the best way to handle this?"

# RECOGNIZING THE CUES

*When you are talking with someone, learn to notice which thinking style – visual, auditory, or kinesthetic (feelings) – is predominant at any particular moment. Recognize the cues so that you can fine-tune your communication to fit their style.*

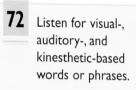

**72** Listen for visual-, auditory-, and kinesthetic-based words or phrases.

**73** Learn to recognize eye movement cues automatically.

## SPOTTING THE CUES

Eye movements and words are clues as to whether someone is thinking in images (Visual style), sound (Auditory style), or feelings (Kinesthetic style). These cues are usually momentary, and people are often unaware of the phenomenon. Generally, when people look up, they are thinking visually. When they look down to their left, they are talking to themselves. When they look down to their right, they are in touch with their feelings. If someone says "I see...", this suggests visual thinking.

**INTERPRETING EYE-ACCESSING CUES ▼**

*Develop your people skills by looking for eye cues that give you insights into how people are thinking. Do this regularly until you start to spot cues automatically.*

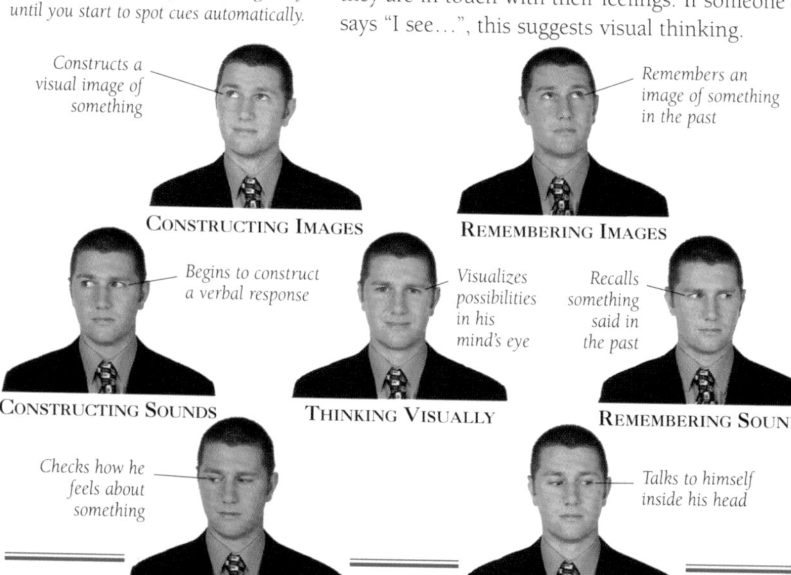
Constructs a visual image of something
CONSTRUCTING IMAGES
Remembers an image of something in the past
REMEMBERING IMAGES
Begins to construct a verbal response
CONSTRUCTING SOUNDS
Visualizes possibilities in his mind's eye
THINKING VISUALLY
Recalls something said in the past
REMEMBERING SOUNDS
Checks how he feels about something
EXPERIENCING FEELINGS
Talks to himself inside his head
INTERNAL DIALOGUE

### POINTS TO REMEMBER

- If you match people's preferred communication system, you avoid treading on people's ears!
- You can learn the skill of changing your thinking style to match whoever you are talking to.
- When you talk to a group of people, use verbal, auditory, and kinesthetic cues equally.

## ADAPTING TO THE CUES

Learn to change your thinking style to match other people's. If a colleague keeps looking up and uses visual words, adapt to a visual-communication style. For example, if they say, "This project is not looking too bright", say, "Let's throw some light on it". If a customer looks down to their left and says, "I'm not sure about this", realize he or she may be talking internally about his or her concerns. Let them know you are happy to talk it through.

## RECOGNIZING LANGUAGE TYPES

| TYPE | EXAMPLES IN SPEECH |
|---|---|
| VISUAL | ● "Bright idea."<br>● "We're not seeing the whole picture."<br>● "We need to focus on another issue." |
| AUDITORY | ● "Sounds good."<br>● "We need to talk this through."<br>● "What he is saying does not ring true." |
| KINESTHETIC | ● "I'm overloaded."<br>● "It feels right."<br>● "I am going to smooth it out." |

## SEEING OTHERS THINK

Thinking is made up of sequences, or "strategies", of images, sounds, and feelings. Spot the cues of people's thinking strategies. For instance, if your boss makes decisions by looking over different options, asking which is the best, and going on his gut feeling, take note of this for when you present him with a new project. For example, say, "Here are the possibilities I've *looked* at. Can we *discuss* which is best until you *feel* we've got the right one."

**74** Spot thinking strategies so you can achieve the best from your staff and your organization.

# INFLUENCING THROUGH LANGUAGE

*Effective communication will impact on your results. Recognize when to be specific with questions, and how to adapt to other people's language patterns so that you can effectively influence them. Aim to understand people's non-verbal responses.*

**75** Realize that by asking questions, you can direct the conversation.

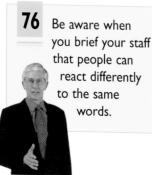

**76** Be aware when you brief your staff that people can react differently to the same words.

## SUCCEEDING THROUGH LANGUAGE

A manager will spend an average of eight minutes on each one-to-one interaction with an employee. What you say in this time is crucial to overall performance and results. Learn to recognize when your words get you the results you want, and when they do not. Be clear about what you want to achieve before you speak. Then compare the result your words actually produced with the result you had intended. Notice when you have to tailor the wording to suit the individual.

## CHOOSING YOUR WORDS

Most of the time, the words you use work very well, but in some interactions you must choose your words carefully. Before these conversations, imagine watching yourself talking with the other person. Then, think through your options. Imagine the response you think they will have to each one. If they respond well in your imagination, then you know what to say to them. If they do not, imagine different approaches until you find one that works. Practise this approach several times in your mind before actually having the conversation.

**77** Use sensitive and thoughtful language.

**78** Learn to read people's responses as you talk.

## ASKING QUESTIONS

Performance is affected by the ability of yourself and others to ask the right questions at the right time. Your team may assume that you know more about an issue than you do, and you may feel uncomfortable about asking. If you are not clear on something, decide on the question you want to ask and when to ask it. When you receive a response, it may be necessary to clarify key words (using the Meta Model), to make sure you fully understand.

### QUESTIONS TO ASK YOURSELF

- **Q** What is the most useful question to ask next?
- **Q** What are we trying to achieve here?
- **Q** What have we not noticed yet?
- **Q** What do we need to change or do differently?
- **Q** What would happen if we did this?
- **Q** What is stopping us from doing this?

### NON FACE-TO-FACE COMMUNICATION

Some people find it difficult if they cannot see the person they are talking to, and find face-to-face communication easier. Before you send e-mails, read them as if you were the recipient. On the telephone, listen closely to responses and changes in voice tone.

**79** Teach yourself and your staff to ask clarifying questions.

## FORMULATING CLARIFYING QUESTIONS (META MODEL)

| STATEMENT | KEY WORD TYPE | QUESTION TO ASK |
|---|---|---|
| "You must always write *reports* better in future." | NOUN | "Which specific reports do you want me to write better?" |
| "You must always *write* reports better in future." | VERB | "How specifically do you want me to write these reports better?" |
| "You *must* always write reports better in future." | RULE | "What will the consequences be if I do not improve them?" |
| "You must *always* write reports better in future." | GENERALIZATION | "Do you really mean you always want me to write them better?" |
| "You must always write reports *better* in future." | COMPARISON | "In what way do you mean better exactly?" |

## REPEATING KEY WORDS

Remember that words can mean different things to different people. Listen carefully to the exact words others use – note their key words as they talk, and then use their key words in response. This will ensure that you communicate in a way that makes sense to them. Do not translate words they use. If someone says, "business performance", avoid changing it to "organizational success" because you think that is what they mean. It may not be.

### POINTS TO REMEMBER

- Translating the words other people use may inadvertently change what they mean.
- Some people may respond to the word "challenge" as something motivating, whereas other people may react to it as a hassle.
- You should always listen carefully for the key words that other people use.

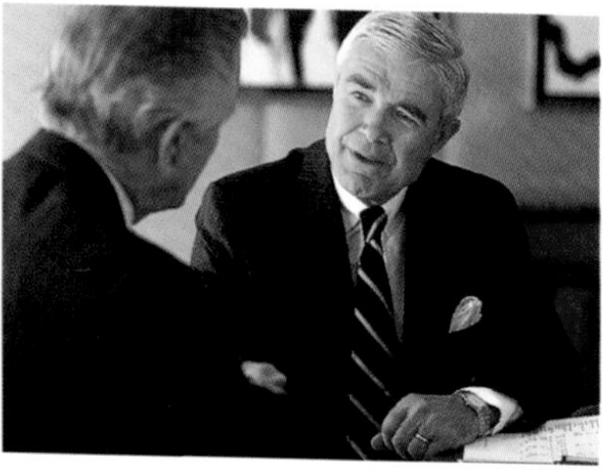

**▲ ASSESSING UNDERSTANDING**
*When you are conversing with people, be sensitive and alert to non-verbal signals so that you can be sure you have been correctly understood.*

## CHECKING FOR SENSE

The verbal part of behaviour is the words that people use. The non-verbal part is the body language and voice tones that tell you how to interpret what is being said. People will tell you non-verbally when what you say makes sense to them and when it does not. If it does, they may signal acknowledgment with a nod. If it does not make sense, the nods will stop, or a facial expression will shift. In this case, rephrase your information, or ask them which bit did not make sense.

**INCREASING ▶ PRODUCTIVITY**
*This case study shows how even subtle changes to people's approach on the telephone can make a huge difference to the response that they get. This is especially important for call centres, which have a high proportion of customer contact.*

### CASE STUDY

The competition that a direct-sales organization faced had increased tenfold over two years. The managing board decided to study the differences between top-performing customer-service staff and the rest. They made some important discoveries. Top performers tended to believe that their job was primarily to help customers. They tended to make a sale only when it was in the customer's interest. This turned a sales job into a service role, which gave the staff a sense of fulfilment. Generally, it was found that top performers would shift their voice tone to try to match the customer's before leading with positive voice tones. They used more of the customer's own language. Based on these findings, the board decided to provide coaching for other staff in these critical skills. The organization's profits doubled within a year.

**80** Empower your staff and benefit from good results.

**81** Look for moments when artfully vague language is useful.

## EMPOWERING OTHERS

If an employee's skills are limited, empower them by spelling out specifically what is required. For example, "We want to maintain a good relationship for future business. I want you to apologise to this customer and offer a full refund." When you deal with highly skilled staff, allow them to come up with their own solutions, so that you empower them to resolve issues in their own way. In this case, artfully vague language (Milton model) often works better than being specific: "Can I leave you to find the best way of dealing with this customer?"

## USING VAGUE LANGUAGE (MILTON MODEL)

| LANGUAGE PATTERN | DESIRED EFFECT |
|---|---|
| "You might have noticed..." | The sentence structure implies that it is okay if they have not noticed the issue. |
| "We're under more competitive pressure..." | This phrasing does not specify who feels what pressure, or how. |
| "You may or may not agree..." | This wording implies that the listeners are free to make their own opinions. |
| "We have to solve problems faster..." | This implies that there is a direct link between the problem and the proposed solution. |
| "Each new problem is an opportunity..." | This phrasing gives a positive angle to an unspecified problem. |
| "Have you already started to wonder..." | This sentence structure encourages people to start thinking. |
| "The challenge will bring out the best in us..." | The wording presents a difficult project as a chance to excel. |

# PROMOTING WINNING IDEAS

*If you want your team to excel, you need to promote productive ideas. Use a strategy for effective thinking by separating the roles of creativity, realism, and criticism from each other and by focusing on these issues at the appropriate time.*

**82** Accept that it will take a lot of ideas to get to a winning one.

▲ **THINKING CREATIVELY**
*If your team members are having trouble being creative, ask them to recall a time when they were resourceful, for example, on an activity weekend.*

## ENCOURAGING CREATIVE THINKING

Avoid criticizing people for creative thinking. Create a space in which people are clear that the aim is to be freely creative without feeling inhibited, and where all ideas are welcomed. Mark out creative thinking time. Ideally, find your own marker. For example, you might make a yellow paper hat with the word "creative" written in large letters. This hat is put on the table to remind others that their job is only to be creative. No criticism is allowed here. Use this marker regularly and people will find it easier to be creative and generate good ideas.

**83** Encourage people to suggest possible improvements.

**84** Check that an idea is realistic and achievable.

### DOS AND DON'TS

- ✔ Do assume that all members of your team have something creative to offer.
- ✔ Do take risks when you feel an idea may be worth pursuing.
- ✔ Do acknowledge and pursue all positive suggestions that your team come up with.
- ✗ Don't criticize creative ideas, or your staff will stop suggesting their views.
- ✗ Don't forget to ask all your team members for their input.
- ✗ Don't assume that others will initiate improvements, as they often will not.

## Thinking Realistically

Once ideas have been generated in the meeting, make it clear that the objective now is to discuss the implementation of ideas. This will reinforce realistic thinking. First, ask "Which are the best ideas?" Take each idea and ask, "How would you implement this?" Ask your team to think through who is doing what, how, and by when. You have a realistic plan when these questions have been answered.

*Sales manager asks her team to look at practicalities of an idea*

**SELECTING IDEAS** ▶

*Once creative ideas have been aired, take the time to sort out the useful ideas from the ones that are not realistic for your organization.*

### Points to Remember

- The creative ideas meeting should be separated from the critical analysis of these ideas.
- Good ideas are not always practical or realistic at first.
- Some ideas may be workable in the future, but not the present.
- Always critically analyze ideas from a number of different points of view to test their feasibility.

## Thinking Critically

If an idea is worth developing, ensure it is robust enough to work. People often get criticized for ideas before they get developed – good ideas are stopped in their tracks. Instead, know when to criticize thinking. In the meeting, make it clear that the purpose now is to troubleshoot. This prevents individuals from taking criticism personally. Then ask, "What is most likely to go wrong?" Allow your team to identify potential issues – the idea may then fail or possible problems be resolved.

## Analyzing Projects

When a project is at the design stage, ensure team members know when to think creatively, critically, and realistically. Notice which role you are weakest at and aim to have someone in your team who is strong in this area. Decide which roles other people are best at. Complement their strengths by taking on their weakest role yourself. Get your team used to thinking and working in terms of these roles.

**85** Form a team who complement each other's strengths and make up for each other's weaknesses.

# CONTINUING TO IMPROVE

Adopting the skills of NLP is an ongoing process of self-development. Nurture the habits of continuous improvement, so that you are empowered to reach your highest potential.

## LIFE PLANNING

*People and organizations that set goals are more likely to achieve them than those that do not. Use regular life planning as an essential tool for keeping yourself on track in a fast-changing world. Treat plans as working directions rather than rigid goals.*

**86** Make a life plan so you can be sure you are working towards your aims.

### CULTURAL DIFFERENCES

Increasingly in the West, people are becoming more interested in working fewer hours and having more time for leisure pursuits. Lifestyle has become a bigger concern than the standard of living. However, in the East, many people are still striving to increase their standard of living.

### DECIDING ON YOUR GOALS

Failing to plan is planning to fail. Constantly think ahead in different areas of your life and over different periods of time so you have a way of keeping yourself on track. Write a list of around seven key life areas down the side of a piece of paper. These might be career, family, finance, health, enjoyment, personal development, and friendships. Choose the areas that suit you. Then, along the top, write different time scales – a month, a year, and five years. Set your own goals for each life area for each time-frame. Make sure you set goals that you are motivated to achieve.

## HARNESSING YOUR MIND

When setting goals, most people under-use the power of their unconscious mind. Learn to get your unconscious mind to work for you. To do this, focus on the difference between your current reality and your goals in order to maintain a creative tension. As long as you do not try to resolve an issue consciously, your unconscious mind will continue to look for a way of resolving the tension. Use this method to help you with life planning.

USING YOUR UNCONSCIOUS MIND ▶
*Many people use meditation as part of their self-development. It can help you focus your mind by letting you observe your thinking processes instead of being caught up in them.*

**87** Realize the power of your unconscious mind – it is the source of your creativity.

*Note down your key life areas*

*Set timescales for achieving your goals*

| Area | 1 Month | 1 Year |
|---|---|---|
| Career | Pay rise | Promotion |
| Family | Short break | Move house |
| Health | Take up cycling | New diet |
| Interests | Read book | New hobby |
| Self | Start diary | Do course |
| Finance | Begin saving | Save 10% |
| Others | Give to charity | Fundraise |

*Set targets for yourself to aim towards in the short- and long-term*

◀ CREATING A LIFE PLAN
*Every 6 months, review and revise your life plan, so that you adapt to changes and ensure that you are still clear on the life you want to lead.*

## USING TIMELINES

Make the goals you set more achievable by imagining that you have already attained them. Look at your life plan as a "timeline", to join your present to your future and past. Take your current location as the present. Imagine the future when you have achieved a goal. Move along the timeline to a goal you set and look back at the present. Walk forward and look back, or do this in your imagination. From the future, see how you achieved a goal.

# ONGOING PERSONAL DEVELOPMENT

*The way to secure long-term career and organizational success is to learn faster than your competitors. Recognize that the fast-track to professional development is to work on your weakest areas, and be honest with yourself about what these are.*

**88** Develop your own personal and professional support systems.

**89** Recognize your weaknesses so you are able to develop.

**90** Make a habit of learning from other people.

## KEEPING A LEARNING LOG

Build the habit of taking 5 minutes every day to review the key incidents of the last 24 hours. First, look at what you did that worked and congratulate yourself. Then look at what did not work. Look at what you would do differently next time. For example, you got really upset when someone blamed you for missing a deadline. On reflection, you realized you wallowed in the injustice of it. Decide that next time you will build in an extra week into the schedule and focus on keeping your emotional state positive.

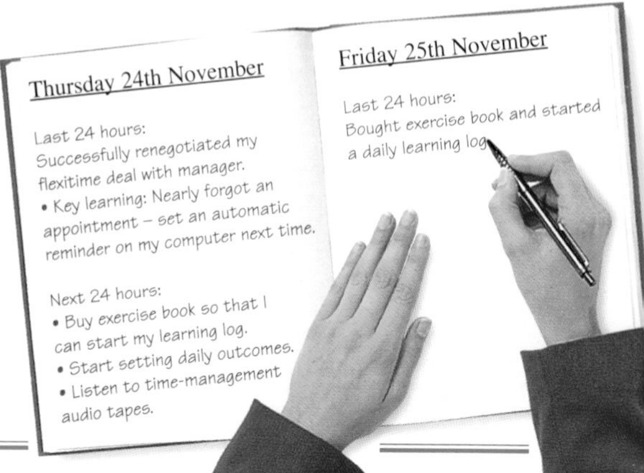

Thursday 24th November
Last 24 hours:
Successfully renegotiated my flexitime deal with manager.
• Key learning: Nearly forgot an appointment – set an automatic reminder on my computer next time.
Next 24 hours:
• Buy exercise book so that I can start my learning log.
• Start setting daily outcomes.
• Listen to time-management audio tapes.
Friday 25th November
Last 24 hours:
Bought exercise book and started a daily learning log


**KEEPING A JOURNAL** ▶
*Make and keep an appointment with yourself every day to write your journal, even if it is only for a couple of minutes. Write down what you achieved that day, and note down areas you need to improve on. This keeps you focused on self-development.*

**THINGS TO DO**

1. Take time to reflect on your development.
2. Always aim to be learning something new.
3. Read papers and journals to keep up to date with developments.

## GETTING STARTED

With a personal-development activity, you must be able to motivate yourself or it will not happen. Consider using a learning log. Getting started is the hard part. When you decide to start, arrange to telephone a friend every day for the first week to let them know whether or not you have done your log for the day. A month after you have started, you may find you are getting stuck on the same issues. Get outside input for new ways of looking at these issues. Find a suitable book, or talk with a friend.

## FINDING YOUR PATH

Personal and professional development is critical to success in business. Look at ways to develop your performance. Decide on the route that works best for you: for example, a one-day course, or an MBA degree. Consider applying for organizational funding. If it is not available, look at spending your own time and money, as an investment in your success. Generally, top performers allocate 10 per cent of their resources to improvement.

**91** Read at least one book a month and create a library that you can refer to in future.

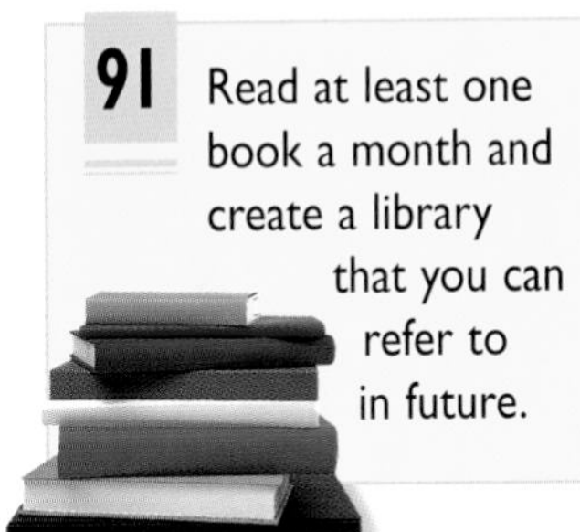

## CHOOSING A PERSONAL-DEVELOPMENT OPTION

| TYPE OF COURSE | ADVANTAGES | DISADVANTAGES |
|---|---|---|
| NLP TRAINING | Complete package of skills for professional success. | The quality of these courses can vary considerably. |
| MBA DEGREE COURSE | A well recognized professional qualification. | This can be expensive and time consuming. |
| TRANSACTIONAL ANALYSIS | Useful for understanding situation dynamics. | These are sometimes not particularly business focused. |
| ONE-DAY BUSINESS COURSE | Courses are tailored to the main business applications. | Changes can be hard to integrate over the long term. |

# COACHING FOR RESULTS

*Top performers recognize they need to continually improve, and use regular coaching to turn weaknesses into strengths. Use coaching to develop these skills and increase your performance. Notice how problems can become opportunities to learn.*

**92** Look at problems as opportunities to concentrate on self-development.

▲ COACHING YOUR STAFF
*Coach your staff to solve their own problems with your support, rather than relying on you for solutions.*

## LEARNING TO SUPPORT

A lot of people think that they can become successful without any support. However, coaching is increasingly used by top managers because it is one of the most effective ways of improving performance. For example, if you find that you procrastinate on sales calls, you can be coached to think of these calls as a chance to build relationships rather than feeling you have to push a sale. Coaching develops your ability to support others and boosts your emotional intelligence. You can then improve your coaching of others.

## JOINING FORCES

To set up a co-coaching system, find a suitable partner and agree to mutual coaching sessions on a regular basis. First, list potential partners – put them in rank order, and approach the highest first. Ask if they are willing to give it a trial run. Decide where and when suits you both best. Then decide how much time to spend coaching each other. Always have equal time each way as coach and coachee.

### DOS AND DON'TS

- ✔ Do reflect on what you would do differently next time.
- ✔ Do informally coach people when situations arise.
- ✔ Do stay calm whatever happens in the session.
- ✘ Don't think you have to know all the answers.
- ✘ Don't interrupt with your suggestions unless asked.
- ✘ Don't criticize people's thoughts and views.

**93** Use coaching time as an opportunity to improve your relationships with your staff.

## DECIDING WHAT TO SAY

As the coachee, focus on whatever it is most useful for you to explore. The session is for you. As coach, your job is to do what is most useful for the coachee. There are three stages to the process: exploring the issue, identifying an outcome or goal, and defining the next action step. As the coach, ask questions until the coachee becomes clearer about the issue, the outcome, and what they are going to do differently. Use your rapport skills to help the coachee feel comfortable and use your enthusiasm to "drive" their emotional state so they are more enthused to take action. At the end, ask the coachee for feedback on what worked, and what you could improve on.

**94** Remember to be supportive and encouraging to your coachee.

**95** Schedule another coaching session, to review the action steps taken.

### USING THE THREE-STAGE COACHING PLAN

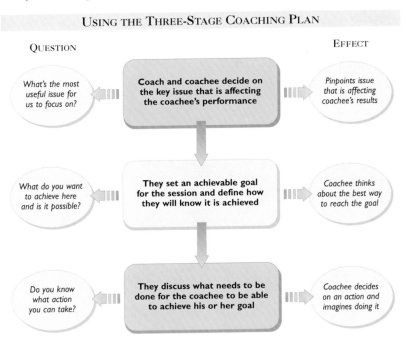

| QUESTION | | EFFECT |
|---|---|---|
| *What's the most useful issue for us to focus on?* | **Coach and coachee decide on the key issue that is affecting the coachee's performance** | *Pinpoints issue that is affecting coachee's results* |
| *What do you want to achieve here and is it possible?* | **They set an achievable goal for the session and define how they will know it is achieved** | *Coachee thinks about the best way to reach the goal* |
| *Do you know what action you can take?* | **They discuss what needs to be done for the coachee to be able to achieve his or her goal** | *Coachee decides on an action and imagines doing it* |

# MODELLING HIGH FLYERS

*Speed up your own development by identifying the key skills you need and by learning them from the people who have them by replicating, or modelling, their habits. Realize that your organization will benefit from the sharing of the most valuable skills.*

**96** Understand that performance is a combination of competencies.

**97** Model the skills of top performers, to improve yourself.

**98** See that emulating others is how you learnt as a child.

## MODELLING THE BEST

High flyers do not reinvent wheels unnecessarily. Understand that performance is a combination of competencies that you can develop. Use NLP to deconstruct skills, such as decision making or delegation, into their component learnable skills. First, find a "model" who is particularly good at the competency you want. This may be someone you already know. If necessary, ask several people's opinions before deciding who to choose as a model. Realize you can learn anything from anyone if you want to, believe you can, and know how to.

## LEARNING HOW

Explain to your model that you have noticed how good he or she is at a skill and ask for a little of their time. Aim to find out what your model is doing differently to you, so you can change what you currently do to improve your results. Look at differences in his or her beliefs, emotional states, and strategies for thinking about and achieving the results he or she gets. Note down the differences between your model and yourself.

Employee asks questions about the relevant skill
Model recalls an example of when he used the skill well

▲ **HAVING A MODELLING INTERVIEW**
*An employee asks a model to recall a time when he used a skill well. She asks him why the skill is useful, what his state of mind was while he was doing it, and what his steps of thinking were.*

## DUPLICATING RESULTS

Once you know what a top performer does differently from you, begin to replicate their skills. Identify which factors make the most difference – imagine doing each one in turn and notice how much impact it has on your performance level. Imagine putting these main sub-skills together. If they work when you mentally rehearse, then begin to practise them for real. If they do not work, ask your model about any factors that are not yet clear. Then apply the new version repeatedly in real life.

### POINTS TO REMEMBER

- Take every opportunity to learn from people you work with.
- Be willing to give time to others who want you to be a role model.
- Constantly look at new ways of improving your performance and your results.
- When you accept that you do not know something, you are ready to learn.

### APPROACHING A MODEL

How you approach your model will affect the response you get. Choose an approach that works best for you. For example:

- "I've noticed that you're very good at presentations. Could I have a few minutes of your time to ask some questions?"
- "I liked the way you handled that client. Would you mind if I talked to you about that?"
- "I've got a problem with a client. Someone told me you would be a good person to talk to. Would that be okay?"

**99** Remember that continuous learning is essential if you are to stay ahead.

### IMPROVING ORGANIZATIONAL PERFORMANCE WITH MODELLING

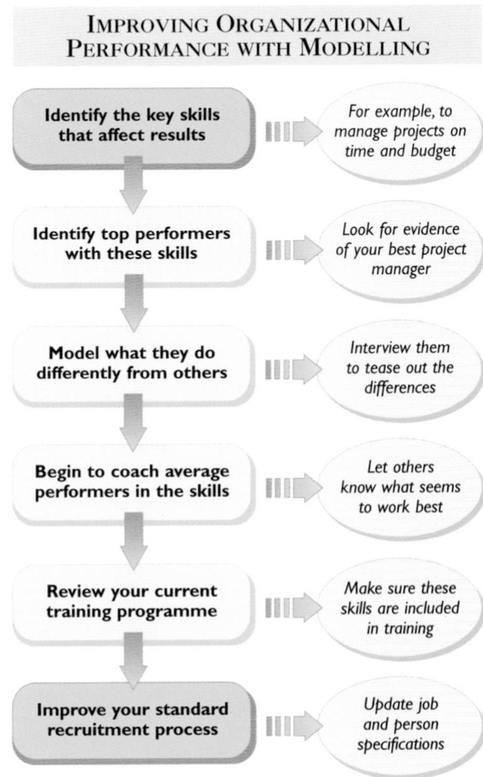

Identify the key skills that affect results
For example, to manage projects on time and budget
Identify top performers with these skills
Look for evidence of your best project manager
Model what they do differently from others
Interview them to tease out the differences
Begin to coach average performers in the skills
Let others know what seems to work best
Review your current training programme
Make sure these skills are included in training
Improve your standard recruitment process
Update job and person specifications

# Developing Leadership Qualities

*Increasingly, NLP skills are being used to develop leadership qualities for personal and organizational success. Recognize that natural leaders have the ability to inspire and bring out the best in others, and that you too can learn to develop these qualities.*

**100** Find role models so you continue to improve your abilities as a leader.

**101** Concentrate on developing your leadership skills so you can perform as a leading-edge manager.

## Managing to Lead

We live in a world of shrinking workforces and rapid change. As a result, the managerial role is changing. There is less focus on giving orders, and more focus on leadership and coaching to bring out the best in employees. Recognize that, through skilful leadership, ordinary people can produce extraordinary results. NLP skills give you the means to become a more effective leader. Think of yourself as a leader and imagine how you would behave differently as you become a more effective leader.

## Leading Yourself

Start to learn the skills of leading yourself by setting yourself compelling goals and being responsible for achieving them. Welcome circumstances that stretch your skills, seek out better ways of doing things, and constantly strive to recognize and work on your weaknesses. Do this by having mentors and by using coaching sessions to develop your skills. Aim to find ways of enjoying every work project that you have. Learn to love your work, especially if you believe this is impossible.

▲ **CELEBRATING SUCCESSES**
*Enjoy your colleagues' company and build up a good rapport. Reward yourself and your team for triumphs, to help encourage successes in the future.*

# LEADING OTHERS

Once you have developed leadership qualities in yourself, you will be able to lead others effectively. Remember, there is nothing that a small group of committed individuals cannot achieve. Learn to inspire and develop vision in others by appealing to their values and interests. Compulsively seek improvements and implement new initiatives and procedures. Empower others to act by giving them the resources and responsibility to deliver results. Achieve credibility by setting a good example, and lastly, reward achievements and give encouragement.

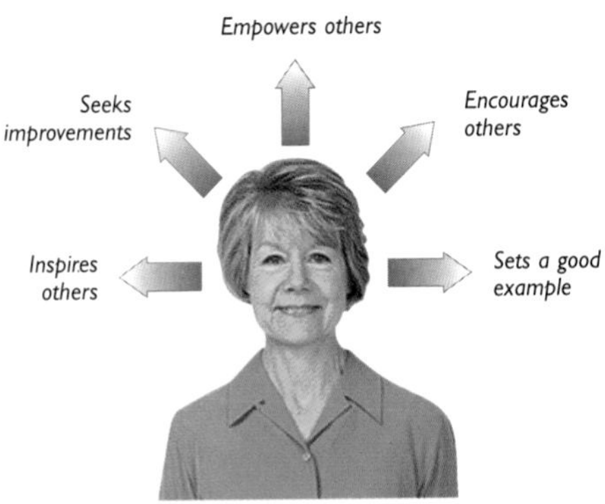


▲ **LEADERSHIP QUALITIES**

*To be a leader, you must earn the respect of others. Recognize the five qualities that all great leaders embody, and work on developing these in yourself.*

## SOLVING PROBLEMS WITH EFFECTIVE LEADERSHIP

| PROBLEM | SOLUTION | MANAGER'S INTERVENTION |
|---|---|---|
| An employee feels a lack of motivation. | Focus on vision and motivation. | Find out more about what matters most to them. Clarify positive values and find creative "win-win" ways to satisfy these. |
| An employee feels a problem is inevitable. | Focus on seeking improvements. | Implement new approaches to get everybody thinking about and suggesting improvements. Act on the best suggestion. |
| Your team talk about what they cannot do. | Focus on empowering staff. | Find out what skills and resources they would need in order to carry out what they would like to do and explore ways of making them possible. |
| Staff do not believe you do as you say. | Focus on teaching by example. | Only say what you mean and always follow through on it. Whatever you ask of others, make sure you are willing to do yourself. |
| Staff feel their work is not valued. | Focus on giving encouragement. | Aim to frequently catch people doing the right things. Develop a wide range of ways to acknowledge and appreciate their work. |

# EVALUATING YOUR PERFORMANCE SKILLS

*Evaluate your ability to maximize performance with NLP by responding to the following statements, and mark the option that is closest to your experience. Be as honest as you can: if your answer is "never", mark Option 1; if it is "always", mark Option 4, and so on. Add your scores together, and refer to the Analysis to see how you scored. Use your answers to identify areas that need improving.*

**OPTIONS**

1 Never
2 Occasionally
3 Frequently
4 Always

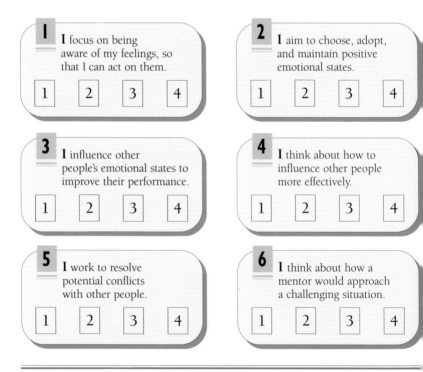

**1** I focus on being aware of my feelings, so that I can act on them.

1 2 3 4

**2** I aim to choose, adopt, and maintain positive emotional states.

1 2 3 4

**3** I influence other people's emotional states to improve their performance.

1 2 3 4

**4** I think about how to influence other people more effectively.

1 2 3 4

**5** I work to resolve potential conflicts with other people.

1 2 3 4

**6** I think about how a mentor would approach a challenging situation.

1 2 3 4

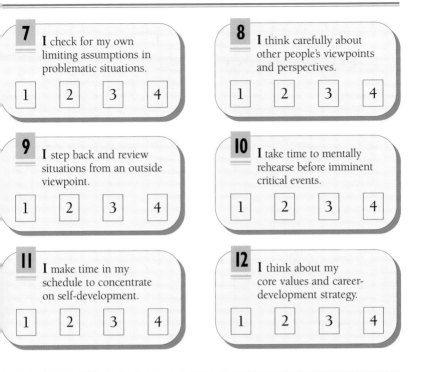

**7** I check for my own limiting assumptions in problematic situations.

1 2 3 4

**8** I think carefully about other people's viewpoints and perspectives.

1 2 3 4

**9** I step back and review situations from an outside viewpoint.

1 2 3 4

**10** I take time to mentally rehearse before imminent critical events.

1 2 3 4

**11** I make time in my schedule to concentrate on self-development.

1 2 3 4

**12** I think about my core values and career-development strategy.

1 2 3 4

## ANALYSIS

Now you have completed the self-assessment, add up your total score and check your performance by referring to the corresponding evaluation below. Whatever level of performance you have achieved, there is always room for improvement. Identify your weakest areas and refer to the relevant sections in this book to develop and hone your NLP skills.

**12–24:** You have considerable potential for improving your performance by using NLP skills to boost your managerial capabilities.

**25–36:** You clearly have strengths and will benefit considerably from concentrating on developing your weakest areas.

**37–48:** You have unusually strong emotional-intelligence capabilities but, to become a real high flyer, you must keep developing your skills.

# INDEX